MATRIMONY, INC.

From Personal Ads to Swiping Right,
A Story of America Looking for Love

FRANCESCA BEAUMAN

PEGASUS BOOKS
NEW YORK LONDON

MATRIMONY, INC.

Pegasus Books, Ltd.
148 W. 37th Street, 13th Floor
New York, NY 10018

Copyright © 2020 by Francesca Beauman

First Pegasus Books edition October 2020

Interior design by Maria Fernandez

Library of Congress Cataloging-in-Publication Data is available.

ISBN: 978-1-64313-578-6

10 9 8 7 6 5 4 3 2 1

Printed in the United States of America
Distributed by Simon & Schuster
www.pegasusbooks.com

CONTENTS

Introduction

⚜

I met my husband through a personal ad.

"Tall-ish, blonde-ish, 28, likes books and pubs and India," was how he described himself. He said he was looking for "an unneurotic brunette." The ad appeared in the *Observer* newspaper, which at the time we both read religiously, one dreary Sunday around the turn of the last century.

After we'd dated for a while, I took the decision to throw my lot in with him permanently. Like any marriage, it was a huge leap of faith. I knew I adored him at dinner and at parties and at brunch with my parents, but I truly gave no thought to the practical stuff like how he would handle a house move or a newborn.

Why? What led me to choose him? (I mean, apart from the fact that I was in love with him, obviously.)

Was it a chemical reaction?

Was it genetic memory?

Was it my subconscious weighing up a range of relevant criteria? We are both from families of five children, for example, which manifests itself most obviously in our ability to eat fast and talk loudly, often at the same time.

Mate choice remains, in many ways, a mystery.

⚜

It is entirely untrue that I met my husband through a personal ad—alas, because it would have satisfied the narrative so neatly.

In fact, I met him at work. I was the host of a television show he was directing. It was my first job in a studio and I was a bit vague about how microphones worked. During breaks, I would dutifully cover my microphone, but it turned out this was not enough to prevent my merry discussion with my costar about the many charms of this director from being broadcast to the entire gallery: the sound mixer, the producer, and the rest of the (almost all male) team.

But perhaps the facts do not entirely matter. The art of advertising is creating a fantasy world: life as we want it to be. Young? Rich? Gorgeous? The kind of bold statements found in consumer ads are often straight up fabrication and fantasy. But when it comes to personal ads, they may not exactly be lies, but they often prove to be not entirely truthful either.

I easily could have met my husband through advertising, after all—most likely through advertising online. Heterosexual couples in the United States are now more likely to meet each other on the Internet than in any other way; a 2019 study by Stanford University found that 39 percent of heterosexual couples met through a dating website or app, versus 27 percent in a bar or restaurant, 20 percent through friends, and 11 percent at work.

Dating websites and apps are the most recent iteration of what we used to call personal ads, which have long been a passion of mine. Ever since I was old enough to appreciate the pleasures of reading the Sunday papers, I have always turned to the personal ads first. I can still remember some of my favorites: "Woman who likes pasta wants man who likes sauce." "Grumpy, poor, complicated man seeks same but prettier." Each one is its own tiny detective story, asking the reader to unravel the intimate mysteries held within.

As I began to research these ads, however, I found they dated back much further than most people realized. America's first genuine marriage ad appeared in the *Boston Evening Post* in 1759. A gentleman advertised for "Any young lady, between the age of eighteen and twenty-three, of a middling stature, brown hair, of good Morals . . ." The city of Boston, along with most of the East Coast, experienced enormous growth in the mid-18th century, creating a society where it was no longer enough to rely on your mother or your neighbor or your pastor to match you up. The generations-old social networks from across the ocean were no help either in this New World. With the launch of the country's first newspapers therefore came the first opportunities to reach out to a wider social circle in search of a spouse.

An examination of 18th- and 19th-century newspapers reveals the existence of personal ads in every state in the nation. From Wisconsin to Wyoming, from Kansas to California, the headline "Wife Wanted" and, later, "Husband Wanted," became a familiar sight. Taken together, they constitute an extraordinary body of evidence about the history of our hearts' desires.

These ads provided a vital service, particularly for white settlers on the American frontier. The homesteading land policies of the U.S. government encouraged marriage by making it hugely financially worthwhile: with just an "I do," you could get 640 acres of land and a working partner. "So anxious are our settlers for wives that they never ask a single lady her age. All they require is *teeth*," declared a correspondent for the *Dubuque Iowa News* in 1838 in a state where men outnumbered women three to one. Further west, in California after the Gold Rush, the gender disparity was even more extreme: two hundred men for every woman. Geographical isolation, as well as rising romantic expectations, led many to conclude that the only sensible way to find a wife and thus start a family was to turn to the newspapers for help.

The American frontier has been the subject of extensive study, including its dire shortage of women. Yet very little research has been done into one of the most effective ways the problem was solved: personal ads. These were crucial to fulfilling America's Manifest Destiny and settling the West: couple by couple, shy smile by shy smile, letter by letter from a dusty, exhausted miner in California to a bored, frustrated seamstress in Ohio. It is a glimpse into the making of modern America, one hundred words of typesetter's blurry black ink at a time.

Between 1820 and 1860, the United States changed faster than in any comparable period before or since: its borders reached the Pacific, its settled area doubled, the number of states increased from eighteen to thirty-three, and there were astonishing improvements in everything from communication to transport. Population growth in urban areas led to an ever-increasing need for personal ads, which reached the height of their popularity around the 1870s. According to one gentleman in Chicago, "My circle of acquaintances is rather limited, so am obliged to adopt this course, in which I wish to act with honor," while "A comely and courtly bachelor in the prime of life and robust health" explained that his "steadfast devotion to an enterprise remote from the beau monde for some years calls for this expedient."

The thousands of ads that appeared in the *New York Times*, the *New York Herald*, and other newspapers provide an insight into the romantic imagination of the kind of men who would surely never express such intimacies elsewhere. New York City's first personal ad in 1788 was from a man looking for a woman who was "under 40, not deformed." Others sought "a well-shaped head" or "clean skin, a sweet breath, with a good set of teeth." Within a hundred years, in the words of Mark Twain, "You may sit in a New York restaurant in the morning for a few hours, and you will observe that the very first thing each man does, before ordering his breakfast, is to call for the *Herald*—and the next thing he does is to look at the top of the first column and read the 'Personals.'"

Single women who answered a "Wife Wanted" ad took an enormous risk traveling 2,000 miles to marry a man they'd never met in a state they'd never visited. Writing letters back and forth was one way to try to vet a prospective amour in advance, but it still offered no guarantees that he was a safe or sensible choice. Yet it often represented the only route to financial security. Answering a personal ad was one of the few ways that women in this period were able to take control of their own destiny. For new immigrants in particular, the ads were a shot at a new life.

From the 1840s onward, as the American female population became increasingly educated and middle-class, the national conversation turned toward the issue of women's rights. The first women's rights convention took place in Seneca Falls, New York, in 1848; around the same time, women began to place their own personal ads. "I want no brainless dandy or foppish fool, but a practical man who can drive a coach or rock the cradle, hoe the garden or attend the ball-room," one informed readers of a Wisconsin newspaper in 1855. Women of this sort generally did not leave behind diaries or letters and had few opportunities to define or manifest themselves other than as an appendage to men; their ads are a rare and valuable example of female desires—some immensely practical, some less so—being committed to paper. A woman in Mandan, North Dakota, wrote to the local paper looking for a second husband just a couple of days after she buried her first husband: "It is coming on spring now, and I am a lone woman with a big ranch and the Indians about. I don't mind the Indians, the red devils, but I have too much work for any woman to do . . ."

By 1880, marriage ads could be found in every state in the nation. In 1885, six African American miners' wives in the towns around Tucson, Arizona, founded the Busy Bee Club and placed ads in African American newspapers across the Eastern seaboard, hoping to persuade others to join them and increase the racial diversity on the frontier. I have been frustrated, however, by the paucity of evidence of other personal ads placed by minority groups. This is in large part due to the many economic and social obstacles that precluded minorities from placing a personal ad (lack of money, lack of time, and, of course, lack of actual freedom for African Americans prior to the emancipation in 1865), as well as the fact that some minorities were more likely to place them in newspapers in their country of origin rather than in the United States and hence they are more difficult to source, but it does mean that the ads featured here disproportionately reflect the white experience.

There was also a dark side to the personals. In 1908, Belle Gunness was discovered to have murdered over forty men at her farmhouse in Indiana, having lured them there using personal ads she placed in newspapers all over the Midwest: "Comely widow . . . desires to make the acquaintance of . . ." the ads began. In this way Gunness earned herself the dubious honor of America's most prolific female serial killer. Despite this, personal ads mostly remained a widely used matchmaking technique, simply due to demand.

What is it about American society that created, and continued to create, such a demand for advertising for love? I argue that, just like possessing a postal service or a sewer system, it is a crucial element of any industrialized, modern, forward-thinking society, which needs personal ads in order to bring its young men and young women together if they find themselves, for a variety of reasons, no longer able to rely on parents, friends, or neighbors to assist them in meeting a domestic partner.

Most of the research for this book involved months of trawling through old newspapers. It was a constant battle not to get distracted by a nearby article about a bizarre murder or a momentous event. I also started to obsess about what happened next to "my" advertisers. Which of these brave souls found themselves a husband or wife, a lover, a friend? Part of the fun of personal ads is they allow the reader to indulge in a little fantasy. Who was the advertiser? What did they look like? Having exposed a part of themselves to the public gaze, what had they kept private? Advertising for love has always been as much about what is not said as what is.

It remains a perennial frustration that we do not know how most of these stories turned out. The way the advertisers disappear from view just as quickly and suddenly as they appear—well, it is the nature of the (semi-anonymous) beast. It has been possible to trace only a few of those whose fate was determined by an ad in a newspaper they read over coffee, tea, Norwegian brew, or Italian pizza, in large part due to the social stigma that used to be associated with meeting your partner this way. The level of stigma has fluctuated over time, but lurking behind many an ad is a Groucho Marx dynamic: whoever is placing it only really wants to meet the kind of person he or she imagines wouldn't be caught dead responding to it.

The 20th century saw a revolution in the way we advertise for love. The first computer dating site, Operation Match, appeared in 1965; thirty years later came Internet dating sites such as Match.com. The likes of Tinder, the location-based dating app launched in 2012 that allows users to swipe right to "like" another user, then matches them up if the feeling is mutual, transformed matchmaking yet again. Next time you swipe right, however, remember that single young men and women have been engaged in a similar process, just via different methods and media, for nearly three hundred years.

According to evolutionary biologist Gil G. Rosenthal, there are a large number of constants in human mate choice: "Evolutionary psychology tells us that men want young, nubile women with symmetrical breasts, clear skin, child-bearing hips, and red lips. . . . Women want square-jawed, testosterone-filled he-men when they're ovulating; and wealthy, compliant protectors when they're not." Within this, however, "Humans harbor tremendous variation in what we find attractive or arousing, and this variation is shaped by environmental, social, and genetic influences." There is also the matter of human agency—free will, even—as well as differences in how we choose a short-term mate compared to a long-term mate, where social and cultural factors come into play more strongly.

What I wanted to know was whether the historical record bears this out. By comparing the content offered up on today's dating apps and websites with centuries-old personal ads placed in newspapers and magazines, it is possible to answer some crucial questions about mate choice in America. What do women look for in a man? What do men look for in a woman? And how has this changed over the past two hundred and fifty years?

William

Watertown, Massachusetts, 1765

I'd known three women my whole life: my mother, my grandmother, and the pastor's wife.

It meant I had plenty of time to work. In the evenings, I swam in the river or rode my horse toward the sunset. Sometimes I read the Bible.

But then they all died of smallpox in the same week.

There was an epidemic, you see. And even though we lived miles from town, it found us.

Never had I known such loneliness. To exist without touch, without warmth, without love—it was to exist not at all.

But when I opened my eyes to the young women around me or in town, well, a new friendship seemed impossible.

I owned a business and I was a kind man; honest, too, and not a drinker, nor did I chew tobacco or use my fists. But I was not a talker, either. Women made me nervous.

I knew how to write though. And the newspaper office was only a half hour gallop away.

And so, I decided to place an advertisement.

CHAPTER ONE

"ANY YOUNG LADY": BOSTON, C. 1720–1760

On February 23, 1759, the front page of Friday's *Boston Evening Post* greeted readers with an account of the latest skirmishes in the Seven Years' War. The owner of a brown leather purse lost last Friday offered a reward for its return and there was an announcement that a brig named the *Hannah* had just docked, bringing with it supplies of cutlery, shoes, and raisins, all now for sale on Third Street.

Meanwhile, nestled unobtrusively on page three, was this:

Boston Evening Post, *February 23, 1759*

It was America's first personal ad (or at least, the first for which evidence still exists).

The advertiser gives little away about himself, offering only that he is "a Person who flatters himself that he shall not be thought disagreeable by any Lady" who meets his criteria. Was he a government officer, so busy at work that he did not have time to meet single, young women? A soldier, new in town? Or perhaps a merchant, already steeped in the practices of buying and selling.

Whatever his profession, it is highly likely that he was British. England's first personal ad was published on July 19, 1695. On page three of one of the weekly pamphlets for sale on the streets of the capital at the time, surrounded by advertisements for a cobbler's apprentice, an Arabian stallion, and a second-hand bed, was this brave plea:

> A Gentleman about 30 Years of Age, that says he had a Very Good Estate, would willingly Match himself to some Good Young Gentle-woman that has a Fortune of 3000l. or thereabouts, and he will make Settlement to Content.

In the years that followed, many similar ads appeared in the London press, copies of which found their way across the Atlantic Ocean in coat pockets and battered trunks and likely provided an excellent source of ideas and inspiration.

To place his personal ad, our advertiser would have had to make his way through the streets of downtown Boston to the newspaper's offices. At the time, Boston was the most civilized, sophisticated, and modern city in the nation, as well as the largest (although it would be overtaken by both New York and Phila-delphia within twelve months). The year the ad appeared, an English clergyman named Andrew Burnaby offered his impressions of the city:

> Boston, the metropolis of Massachusetts-Bay, in New England, is one of the largest and most flourishing towns in North America. . . . The length of it is nearly two miles, and the breadth of it half a one; and it is supposed to contain 3000 houses, and 18 or 20,000 inhabitants . . . The buildings in Boston are in general good. The streets are open and spacious, and well-paved; and the whole has much the air of some of our best country towns in England. . . . The chief public buildings are three churches, thirteen or fourteen meeting-houses,

the governor's palace, the court-house or exchange, Faneuils-hall, a linen-manufacturing-house, a work-house, a bridewell, a public granary, and a very fine wharf . . .

Passing all this infrastructure, the advertiser would have nervously found his way to the sign of the Heart and Crown on Cornhill (now Washington Street), arriving at a grand townhouse belonging to Thomas Fleet, the publisher of the *Boston Evening Post*. The newspaper's offices were on the ground floor.

Why Boston? Well, its print media was the most advanced in the nation, its population the most literate. The average print run of each of the city's three weekly newspapers (the *Boston Evening Post*, the *Boston News-Letter*, and the *Boston Gazette*) was about six hundred copies, but their readership was far higher because every edition was passed around coffeehouses and taverns for days.

Did the clerk at the front desk of the *Boston Evening Post*'s offices raise an eyebrow when our advertiser presented his ad? Did he hand it directly to Thomas Fleet, knowing that Fleet would have been delighted by its entertainment value? In any case, by commercializing matchmaking, the *Boston Evening Post* brought marriage into line with rooms to rent, a horse for sale, the arrival of tea from the Indies—the provision of yet another service to meet the demands of recently settled colonists.

The ad contains a rare public declaration of what an 18th-century gentleman looked for in a wife. To wit: "Any young Lady, between the Age of Eighteen and Twenty-three, of a middling Stature; brown Hair; regular Features, and with a lively brisk Eye; of good Morals, and not tinctur'd with any Thing that may sully so distinguishable a Form; possessed of 3 or 400l., entirely at her own Disposal."

In other words: young, respectable, and rich.

Yet some of the other criteria merit further attention. Why "brown Hair," for example? Perhaps he had recently had a painful experience with a blonde. He was also specifically seeking a woman whose wealth was "entirely at her own Disposal, and where there will be no necessity of going thro' the tiresome Talk of addressing Parents . . ." which reflects the strict control that New England parents still exerted over their children, a reason why personal ads did not take off faster than they did.

Advertising for a mate was so unconventional—to some, so shocking—that the advertiser reassures interested parties that "Profound secrecy will be observ'd," adding that "No trifling answers will be regarded." He was clearly realistic about the high chance of being pranked: while his very public declaration was wonderfully bold and brave, it also made him an easy target for those fearful of innovation.

The advertiser asks anyone interested to leave a note at the British Coffee-House (more evidence that he was English?), one of the most popular coffeehouses in pre-Revolutionary Boston. The membership included officers of the king and lesser officials, military and naval leaders, members of the bar, and other prominent citizens who were friends of the crown. A few years earlier, some British redcoats had staged Boston's first play there.

The pages of a newspaper are relatively democratic: while you needed a few spare shillings to buy an ad, you did not need power, influence, or social status. With this new form of text, anyone could see themselves in the pages of a newspaper. Stacks of newspapers, delivered to coffeehouses and market squares, to rural estates and inns, had the potential to be a powerful tool in mobilizing support for a rebellion against the ruling establishment. The timing was perfect, too, as a newly egalitarian rhetoric began to emerge out of Boston—a rhetoric that would, fifteen or so years later, culminate in revolution.

The day after the marriage ad appeared, a number of gentlemen stopped by the British Coffee-House to hear more about the recent opening of the nation's first life insurance company, while others were there just to read the papers and smoke a cigar. There was perhaps one among them, sitting alone at a corner table, anxiously waiting to see if any letters written in a woman's hand (Scented with rose water? Or is my imagination running away with me?) arrived for his attention. We can only speculate about what happened next. In some ways, though, this is the very essence of the appeal of marriage ads, both then and now: the curious combination of romance and mystery.

⊗

The success of any human society depends upon the ease with which its single, fertile men and women are able to meet and mate. Otherwise, how is anyone supposed to make babies? In the earliest days of America's colonization, ensuring a sufficiently stocked mating pool proved a constant challenge.

In 1607, one hundred and four English men and boys, backed by the Virginia Company, docked at a marshy peninsula about thirty miles up the James River in what is now Virginia. Jamestown became the first permanent English settlement in North America. There was a problem, though. There were no women on the expedition. None at all.

Unsurprisingly, many settlers ending up forming relationships with Native American women, but the racist principles upon which the Virginia Company was governed meant that this was strongly discouraged. The colonial reverend William Symonds referred in one of his sermons to the Bible's instruction that "God's people in Canaan 'keepe to themselves'" and "not marry nor give in marriage to the heathen, that are uncircumcised"; the "breaking of this rule" would risk "all good succese of this voyage."

The first English women arrived in Jamestown in 1608: Martha Forrest, the wife of a settler, and her fourteen-year-old maid, Anne Burras. Not long afterward they were followed by another 120 women on the third supply ship. None, however, were single, and the shortage of eligible women remained a serious problem. As the treasurer of the Virginia Company, Sir Edwin Sandys, put it, ". . . the plantation can never flourish till families be planted and the respect of wives and children fix the people on the soil." The longevity of the colony depended upon men and women having the social support they needed to couple up and so, in 1619, the company ordered that ". . . a fit hundredth might be sent of women, maids young and uncorrupt, to make wives to the inhabitants and by that means to make the men there more settled and less movable . . ." It was corporate matchmaking: the following year, the Virginia Company sponsored 140 single women to make the journey from England for the specific purpose of marrying them off and thereby encouraging the male colonists to remain.

It worked. The marriage rate, then the birth rate, started to increase, and Jamestown flourished, the population rising to nearly 1,400 people by 1622. America's first permanent settlement was, for the meantime, secure.

Over the next century or so, marriage was viewed as the foundation upon which American society was built. With most communities based around the rituals of the Christian church, it was the only context in which sexual relations were officially sanctioned. It was also a matter of economic prudence, both for the working classes that sought to share life's practical burdens and for the middle and upper classes that had property to protect.

With the settlement of New England, the authorities showed themselves keen to increase the population as quickly as possible, promoting marriage however they could. One Connecticut town made it criminal to be a single householder, forbidding "any young unmarried man to keep house." Another imposed a tax of twenty shillings a week on "the selfish luxury of solitary living."

The authorities also attempted to regulate courtship and keep it in line with prevailing Puritan values. A law passed in New Haven in 1656 made it illegal to "inveigle or draw the affections of any maid . . . by speech, writing, message, company-keeping, unnecessary familiarity, disorderly night meetings, sinful dalliance, gifts, or any other way, directly or indirectly."

But it was almost impossible to enforce laws like this. The colonial population was so dispersed that state surveillance was weak; it was instead left up to the local community to police behavior, and they tended to be pragmatic and flexible depending on circumstances. This was why popular courting customs flourished—take bundling, for example.

Bundling was the practice of a couple, sanctioned by their families, messing around in bed fully clothed. It was probably first introduced to the New World by settlers from Holland, where there was a similar ritual known as *queesting*. There were ways of ensuring it did not get out of hand, such as a piece of wood that divided the bed but did not prevent the contact of hands or lips. Some mothers tied their daughters' ankles together or sewed up undergarments in carefully considered places. Bundling made sense in an era when night was the only free time for courting; it also saved on fuel, which was scarce, and on space, when homes were small. (The practice deserved a book of its own and in 1869 Henry Reed Stiles made all our dreams come true with his classic text, *Bundling: Its Origins, Progress and Decline in America*.)

Family and friends tended to have a fair amount of say in a young person's choice of a partner (although there were few arranged marriages in the formal sense). Marriage was primarily viewed as an economic and social alliance. When assessing a potential future husband or wife, the focus was on what he or she could bring to the relationship in cash, property, status, and skills or accomplishments.

In 1689, the philosopher John Locke had proposed a radical new view of marriage in his book *Two Treatises of Government*. He argued that it ought to be a contract between equals:

> Conjugal society is made by a voluntary compact between man and woman; . . . [it] leaves the wife in the full and free possession of what by contract is her peculiar right, and gives the husband no more power over her life than she has over his; the power of the husband being so far from that of an absolute monarch, that the wife has in many cases a liberty to separate from him, where natural right, or their contract allows it.

Locke provided the intellectual framework for the belief that love was more important than money as grounds for marriage. But in New England in the late 17th and early 18th centuries, many were concerned that prioritizing emotion over reason would lead to chaos in the marriage market. Society tends to joke about whatever makes it anxious, and it is therefore no coincidence that America's first satirical marriage ad appeared not long afterward.

The satirical marriage ad had been invented in England, drawing inspiration from other ads of the period in search of a servant or a horse rather than a husband or wife. One of the earliest appeared on May 16, 1660, just as King Charles II informed Parliament that he was willing to accept their invitation to reclaim the throne following the English Civil War. It was a plea in the London magazine *Mercurius Fumugosus* from a "worthy, plump, fresh and willing Widdow" who was urgently in need of "any man that is Able to labour in her Corporation." Bawdy Londoners no doubt found the idea of a sexually voracious widow, "plump" and "fresh" like a chicken waiting to be plucked, hilarious.

America's first satirical marriage ad came about thanks to Benjamin Franklin's older brother, James Franklin. Born in 1697, James was the fourth son of Josiah Franklin and Abiah Folger. As a teenager, he was sent to London to work as a printer's apprentice. On his return, he was hired by Boston's postmaster, who was setting up a newspaper called the *Boston Gazette* and wanted him to run the printing side.

Boston already had two newspapers. The *Boston News-Letter* had been launched in 1704: it was America's first regularly published newspaper and had close ties to the government of Massachusetts. Most of its articles were borrowed from the London press, which meant that news tended to be about three months out-of-date, the duration of an Atlantic crossing.

Early on, the paper put out a call to "all persons who have any Houses, Lands, Tenements, Farms, Ships, Vessels, Goods, Wares or Mechandizes, to be Sold or Let; or Servants Run-Away, or Goods Stole or Lost; may have the same inserted at a reasonable rate, from Twelve Pence to Five Shillings." The result, two weeks later, was America's first paid newspaper ads: one seeking the return of some men's clothing stolen from James Cooper's house, one trying to track down a lost iron anvil, and another about a mill for rent in Oyster Bay, Long Island.

In 1720, the *Boston News-Letter* was joined by the *Boston Gazette*. Similarly staid in tone, it consisted mostly of news, official announcements, and ads—in particular, ads for runaway slaves.

James Franklin saw a market for a newspaper that took a more irreverent approach. Inspired by humorous magazines like the *Tatler* and the *Spectator* that he had read while apprenticing in London, his aim was to challenge the dull, conventional content of the *News-Letter* and the *Gazette*. And so, in the summer of 1721, Franklin took the bold (some said foolish) step of establishing Boston's third newspaper, the *New England Courant*.

According to a later account by Benjamin Franklin, articles in the *Courant* were written not only by his brother but also by "some ingenious Men among his Friends who amuse'd themselves by writing little Pieces for this Paper, which gain'd it Credit, and made it more in Demand." They included Dr. William Douglass, Captain Taylor, John Checkley, Matthew Adams, John Eyre, and a Mr. Gardner. James also employed sixteen-year-old Benjamin as an apprentice.

The literary content of the *New England Courant* was crucial to its success: it carried hardly any advertising and there was no post office business to underpin it, so sales were the only way to make it pay. With this in mind, Franklin went even further than the *Tatler* and the *Spectator* in his determination to annoy the entire political and religious establishment and to scandalize his father's generation along the way. The *Courant*'s highly combative essays and spirited verses targeted Massachusetts's magistrates, clergy, anyone with money or property, and even—shock, horror—Harvard. It became the first newspaper in America to take a truly independent stance and was the most readable of all those published in this period, helping to satisfy a growing urge for free speech and pioneering a distinctively American form of journalism. One of the earliest targets for satire was matchmaking.

April 13, 1722. Sixteen-year-old Benjamin Franklin sat down to breakfast and spread out the latest edition of the *New England Courant* before him. On the front page was an article he had written in the guise of a widow named Silence Dogood about the importance of serving one's country. It was only the third piece of writing Franklin had ever had published, and he perhaps skimmed through it proudly before his eye was drawn to another item a little further down the page:

New England Courant, *April 13, 1722*

The ad was from a "well accomplish'd young widower" looking for a "young gentlewoman (virgin or widow)" to marry. In an accompanying letter, the "widower" claimed to have lost his previous "wife in the latest Calamitous sickness" and was now hunting for a new partner, "being in haste for another money'd Woman," mocking those who married for riches alone.

The "sickness" to which the widower refers was smallpox, which had reached Boston a year earlier in April 1721 aboard the British warship HMS *Seahorse*. By the time the ad appeared, over half the city's population of 11,000 had caught the disease and 14 percent had died from it. The epidemic led to the first vaccinations in American history, pioneered by Reverend Cotton Mather. It also created a large number of widows and widowers, many of whom had (re-)marriage on their mind.

The advertiser is after "Any young Gentlewoman" who "has five or six hundred Pounds, to secure to him by Deed of Gift." At the end of the ad, in case readers were still unsure whether the ad was serious, he instructs interested parties to "repair to the Sign of the Glass-Lantern in Steeple-Square." The phallic reference to "Steeple-Square" is a giveaway that this is a sexual innuendo, poking fun at the kind of men who are overly brazen about wanting a wealthy wife.

The ad was written by a frequent contributor to the *New England Courant* named Mr. Gardner, about whom we know basically nothing. Evidence for his authorship can be found in the British Library in London, which holds one of the few extant original copies of the ad. The library's file of the *New England Courant* is unique. Every issue is covered with pencil marks to indicate who wrote each piece: the initials "BF" are scribbled next to any that we know to be Benjamin Franklin's work, while the other contributors' names are written out in full. The file begins with the first edition and ends in September 1723, the same month Benjamin Franklin left Boston for New York. The only logical conclusion is that the file belonged to Benjamin Franklin himself and that the pencil marks are his.

One of the earliest pieces of satire ever to be published in America, Mr. Gardner's ad highlights the deeply mercenary approach of many aspects of Boston society. In doing so, it implicitly advocates in favor of political self-determination—that is, for a society that values individual merit over birth. It is also evidence of some of the earliest rumblings of rebellion against a colonial establishment that, in the eyes of some Bostonian patriots, had become venal and self-serving. Its very existence suggests a society beginning to find its voice.

It was to be another thirty-seven years before the personal ad on page three of the *Boston Evening Post* looking for "Any young Lady, between the Age of Eighteen and Twenty-three, of a middling Stature . . ." appeared. While there were almost certainly others, this is the only one to survive in the archives. Personal ads remained rare because the traditional matchmaking process was still functioning adequately and there was no need for alternative approaches. The population was small and predominantly rural; most people married the girl or boy next door, or their parents' friends' children, and eight of the thirteen colonies passed laws requiring parental consent for marriage. The gender balance in New England was roughly equal because, from its earliest days, it had been settled mostly by families, rather than single men. Farther south, where the gender balance was more of a problem, the newspaper business was underdeveloped. But then came the Revolution, one side effect of which was that the innovative method of matchmaking introduced to Boston in 1759 by an anonymous, probably British gentleman was to take on a new and important significance all across the country, lasting right up until the present day.

Thomas

New York, 1778

One morning, I woke up under the lathe and decided I had to get married.

Working every hour of the day and night was great for business, but not so great for the soul. Or the body.

I was, however, new in town. I had only a couple of friends and no family. Marriage felt far beyond my capabilities.

Shipping in the colony's first supplies of lace, measuring for dresses with such precision that my tape measure trembled, reassuring the seventeen-year-olds in for the first time that the cut was surely demure enough for their first ball at the Merchant House? Easy; these challenges did not daunt me.

But a wife to share my bed! How on earth . . . ? Meet her at a party, you say? Pah! All the guests were customers of mine and I couldn't risk the relationship. In my workshop, the only women to whom I spoke were the thirteen-year-old girl who delivered the yarn and the ancient laundress who, it turned out, was from the same town as me back in Scotland. And I rarely went to church anymore, so even the vicar couldn't help.

And the fact was, I was shy.

And so, I decided to place an advertisement.

CHAPTER TWO

"Under 40, Not Deformed":
New York, c. 1770–1810

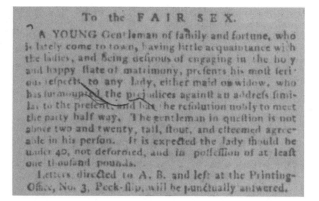

Impartial Gazetteer, *July 23, 1788*

It was the summer of 1788. Delegates at New York's state assembly were in the midst of a heated debate over whether to adopt the nation's new constitution. Inside the courthouse in downtown Poughkeepsie, Alexander Hamilton and John Jay, two of the authors of *The Federalist Papers*, were among those arguing in favor, with Governor George Clinton and others in fierce opposition.

At least one New Yorker, however, had matters of a more personal nature on his mind.

On a humid Tuesday afternoon, a carriage clattered to a halt on Peck Slip in lower Manhattan, outside the offices of the *Impartial Gazetteer*. This was one of half a dozen newspapers published in the city at the time, but the only weekly.

The side door swung open and on to the muddy cobblestones stepped a gentleman who was strangely muffled up, considering the weather. He glanced one way down the street, then the other, then strode inside. He was there to place an ad: not for a horse for sale nor a room to rent, but for a wife. His reference to "the prejudices against an address similar to the present" suggests he felt the need to be discreet.

The advertiser described himself as "a young gentleman of fame and fortune . . . not above two and twenty, tall, stout, and esteemed agreeable in his person." He has chosen to use this "method of address" because he "is lately come to town, having little acquaintance with the ladies."

He is very clear about what he is looking for in a wife. "Under 40, not deformed, and in possession of at least one thousand pounds." This description is almost poetic in its straightforwardness, revealing our bachelor's cheery willingness to consider a wide range of women as long as they are 1) youngish and thus, likely to be fertile; 2) physically healthy, also with fertility in mind; and 3) rich in resources. Although the language used is not quite the same as the kind found on Tinder today, which might read more like "twenty-something, slim, ambitious," it is strikingly similar in its meaning. Translated into evolutionary terms, these criteria are all central tenets of human mate choice.

At 8:00 A.M. the day after our "young gentleman of family and fortune" placed his ad, the city woke to the sound of thirteen guns fired from the federal ship *Hamilton*. It signaled the start of the Grand Federal Procession, a parade through lower Manhattan organized to demonstrate New York's support for the new constitution.

New Yorkers in favor of adopting the constitution believed that the city's continuing economic prosperity depended upon the thirteen states working together, in addition to sharing power with the national government. Around five thousand costumed men from over sixty professions and trades gathered in the rain aboard enormous decorated floats to represent the riches they felt would result from a union.

The bakers were at the front, holding a ten-foot-long "federal loaf"; at the rear were the blacksmiths, banging on an anchor while chanting in unison, "Forge me strong, finish me neat, I soon shall moor a Federal fleet."

The parade increased local support for a union. The following day, the convention in Poughkeepsie voted to ratify the constitution, thirty votes to twenty-seven, the narrowest margin in any state. Federalism had won the day—just.

With all this and a federal loaf to think about, it is probable that our "gentleman of family and fortune" received disappointingly few immediate replies to his ad. All day, huge crowds lined the route and access to the surrounding streets was severely restricted. Any women whose curiosity had been piqued by his ad would have had great difficulty reaching the newspaper office to leave him a letter as requested.

In the days that followed, however, a succession of women—some with entirely sincere motives, others not—could perhaps be seen sneaking down to Peck Slip, which was an active docking area. Dodging crates of freshly caught fish was surely worth it for a shot at married life.

❈

New York's first personal ads emerged out of the chaos of the War of Independence.

In the aftermath of the Battle of Brooklyn in 1776, when New York was captured by the British, joyful Loyalists returned to the city they had fled in fear months earlier. The population was further increased by British troops who were stationed there, as well as by refugees driven out of Patriot areas elsewhere, and within a couple of years it topped 33,000.

The city prospered greatly as a result. British officers needed dressmakers and hatmakers and coach-makers; military equipment was in high demand; trade boomed even with rebel-held New Jersey and Connecticut. The fashionable set had a whirlwind of social events to attend, from saltwater bathing parties to concerts to foxhunting. The City Tavern on Broadway hosted a "Garrison Assembly" every other week, featuring local women dancing with "genuine, smooth-faced, fresh-coloured" Englishmen "of family and consideration," as memorably described by the American prisoner of war Alexander Graydon. It is evidence of a critical mass of young people with both the time and the money to pursue matters of the heart however and whenever they saw fit, regardless of what was happening on the national stage.

Among those who returned to this lively city was James Rivington. The well-educated son of a London bookseller, his newspaper, the *Royal Gazette*, was one of three coming off the printing presses in New York at the outbreak of war, alongside the *New York Journal* and the *New York Gazette*.

Rivington was official printer to the king and continually seeking new ways to persuade the British establishment in New York to make his newspaper their preferred read. (It is alleged that he later switched his allegiance and became a spy for George Washington, but that's another story.) A pattern begins to emerge: combine a thriving literary culture with dramatic population growth, and one result is personal ads.

By January 1778, George Washington's Continental Army was holed up in Valley Forge, a military camp near Philadelphia, for the winter. Conditions were terrible: the men were starving, living in damp, crowded quarters, poorly clothed and ravaged by disease, and Washington had to beg Congress for more supplies. In sharp contrast, life for the Loyalist elite back in New York remained rosy—rosy enough to begin to think about settling down, even. On the last day of the month, the following ad appeared in the *Royal Gazette*:

Royal Gazette, *January 31, 1778*

Above it was an ad for "a handsome black mare, about fourteen hands and an inch high, has a small star on her forehead, and was heavy with foal" that had disappeared from Doctor Charlton's pasture the Monday before; below was a plea for the return of a stolen suitcase.

The advertiser, S.G., describes himself as a "Gentleman of an easy, genteel fortune." The use of the word "genteel," in the sense of well-born, suggests the influence of the many personal ads on display in British newspapers in this period, where it was more frequently used than any other adjective. In New York, a fluid society where everyone was jostling to establish their social credentials, it was an especially powerful identifier.

S.G. explains that he is advertising for a wife, rather than trying to meet one in a more conventional manner, because he is "an absolute stranger to the ladies of this place." One has to admire his boldness. It is also a clue to his identity. Perhaps he was a Patriot who had fled to safety from elsewhere; my hunch is that he was a young blood in the army and, like in Boston almost twenty years earlier, probably British and already familiar with the genre.

S.G. prioritizes just two attributes in his search for a wife: she must be "a lady" and "about 23, 24 or 25 years of age." In other words, respectable and young.

Yet he also asserts the importance of "mutual felicity"—that is, that both parties had a right to the pursuit of happiness, a phrase Thomas Jefferson had written into the Declaration of Independence just eighteen months earlier. A sense was beginning to emerge in America that it was reasonable and in fact sensible to hope to marry for love, or at least amiable companionship, rather than solely for social or economic gain.

It is also noteworthy that S.G. uses the word "honour" once and "honourable" twice; it signals a concern that the unconventional and public nature of his declaration would attract censure and disapproval, rather than single young women.

New York's population continued to grow, and by 1782 it reached 50,000. The following March, peace negotiations got underway in Paris. March 10 saw the last naval battle of the war, fought off the coast of Florida. Three days later, readers of the *New York Packet* were variously shocked and amused to wake up to a personal ad among its pages.

The ad was from by "A Young Gentleman just compleating the twenty third Year of his Age" who went under the moniker Z.J. (not Jay-Z). Men in this period married at an average age of twenty-five and a half (women at twenty-two and a half), so he was nearly but not quite ready to panic. He describes himself as "of a middling Stature, an open, frank and agreeable Countenance, of genteel Mien and Air."

The tone and content of the ad has again been considerably influenced by British personal ads, for example, his claim that he "has a considerable acquaintance with the *Beau Monde*." He underscores his sophistication by noting that his "Travels have not been confined to the Continent only, but who has visited the Gallic Coast."

Z.J. is hoping for a wife who is a "Lady either Maid or Widow, provided her Circumstances will enable them to live in that happy State of Mediocrity, equally removed from the Follies of the Great, and the Vices of the Low; and who may be blessed with the good Nature to wink at the lesser Foibles of human Weakness." The reference to "Circumstances" makes one wonder whether this was in fact the primary motivation behind the ad, but it is of course impossible to know.

The advertiser goes on to lament, "Reflections have taught him to despise the vain Pleasures and idle Follies of the World." New York was becoming known for its decadence and debauchery. Visitors were scandalized by the brazenness of its huge number of prostitutes. The city's governor, sixty-year-old Commandant James Robertson, openly kept multiple mistresses; in Judge Thomas Jones's disapproving account, Robertson could often be spotted "smelling after every giddy girl" and "waddling about town with a couple of young tits about twelve years of age under each arm."

Z.J., like his predecessors, was also on guard against pranks: "As the Writer is sincere, he expects that none from an Idle Curiosity will give themselves any unnecessary Trouble to discover him." He concludes, "A Line directed to Z.J. at Fish-Kill will be properly attended to."

Fish-Kill (now Fishkill), a town in the southwest of Dutchess County, New York, was the site of a military encampment that became the main supply depot for the northern division of the Continental Army. The editor of the *New York Packet*, an Irish immigrant named Samuel Loudon, was forced to move his print shop there in order to escape the British occupation. Once ensconced, Loudon won the contract to be the official state printer and published orders for the Continental Army, issued state currency, and distributed the first copies of the New York State Constitution. He also brought advertising for love outside of the city for the first time.

Such ads continued to appear only sporadically. In 1784, the *Pennsylvania Packet* featured one from "a young Gentleman, just beginning house-keeping." This makes it sound like he was panicking about how to fill the oil lamps or churn the butter, but in 18th-century vernacular it meant he had just moved into his own home. He wanted a wife of "sound wind and limb . . . a clean skin, a sweet breath, with a good set of teeth . . ." (all of which are qualities that indicate fertility). She must also be "Not very talkative, nor one that is dumb; no scold, but of a spirit to resent an affront; of a charitable disposition; not overfond of dress, though always decent and clean; that will entertain her husband's friends with affability and cheerfulness, and prefer his company to public diversions and gadding about . . ." It is stark evidence of the impossible expectations placed on women at the time.

Nonetheless, the ad may have appealed to some. By the 1770s, more than a third of Philadelphia's adult women were unmarried and living in the households of non-relatives. Although the city offered more opportunities for female economic self-sufficiency than anywhere else in the colonies (domestic service, nursing, opening a boarding house or a shop), getting hitched remained almost the only way for a woman to run her own home.

Personal ads were slowly entering the cultural consciousness. In 1799, Isaiah Thomas, a well-known publisher in Worcester, Massachusetts, introduced the novel *Belinda; or, An Advertisement for a Husband* to the new nation. Set in England and written by an anonymous author, it became hugely popular, featuring prominently in booksellers' ads all over the East Coast.

The book is structured in the form of letters from Belinda Blacket to her friend Louisa Lenox, who has recently left London and moved to Northumberland. In the first letter, Belinda confesses her impatience to find a husband. She comes up with a "scheme [that is] is very practicable, though it may be thought to deviate, in some degree, from the delicacy of my sex," explaining that she will place a personal ad:

> Beauty, like any other mercantile commodity, is become an article of traffic in our daily prints; advertisements indiscriminately announce the bargain and sale of a lady's person, or a bale of silk; and direct the readers whither they are to repair to treat for the affections of a lady,

with as little reserve as if she had been a hogshead of sugar, or any other common article of commerce.

Louisa is horrified: "Suffer me to expostulate a little with you, on the impropriety of exposing your person, to the wanton sneers of a rude rabble." Belinda ignores her opinion, places the ad, receives a large number of replies, but ends up marrying a chaplain named Mr. Proby whom she meets elsewhere, concluding that "I candidly acknowledge that the project I engaged in, was a ridiculous one, however fortunate the event."

By the turn of the century, literate New Yorkers were sufficiently familiar with personal ads that it was possible to satirize them and the motives underlying them, just like Bostonians before them. In 1803 a piece appeared in the weekly newspaper the *Museum* under the headline ADVERTISEMENT FOR A HUSBAND. "Maria-Ann" was supposedly on the hunt for a husband who was "tall without being bulky or lean, and pretty tolerably shaped. Religious, without being a hypocrite. Sincere, without a tincture of dissimulation in his composition. He must be neither a beau nor a rake . . ." Try putting that on your Tinder profile.

"Maria-Ann" offers up a detailed description of herself. She includes the memorable boast that "I can dance a few country dances, such as *The humours of Cork, Kiss me quick, my mother's coming, The devil's in't, The great muff*. . ." but is also keen to make sure the world knows that "I don't wear what are commonly called in the fashionable vocabulary of coxcomical hair-cutters, 'Wigs-à-la-Titus.' The hairstyle "à la Titus," named after the Roman emperor, was a short, choppy cut originally popular with men in the aftermath of the French Revolution, later adopted by some women looking to make a political statement in favor of republicanism.

Maria is not done discussing her hair, though: ". . . A giddy head, adorned with dead people's hair, is to be truly disgusting; no, I wear my own hair, which is of an auburn color." Wigs made of "dead people's hair" were indeed popular in this period; her rejection of them in favor of her own natural red hair highlights the supposedly superficial ways in which women defined and differentiated themselves during the matchmaking process.

The mockery was far more sophisticated than the equivalent in Boston eighty years earlier and soon spread beyond New York City to the rest of the state. In 1805, the Sag Harbor newspaper the *Suffolk Gazette* featured a piece from one

"Katy Candour," who offered up a humorous account of what she was looking for in a husband:

> When dull or weary, he must cheer me;
> When I "scold" with patience hear me—
> Must go and come whene'er I bid him,
> And shew contrition when I chide him.

These few lines of verse convey the uneasy tension within the marriage contract in this period. Post–American Revolution, post–French Revolution, "Katy Candour" was not alone in questioning the basis of marriage, along with the traditional gender roles that men and women played within it.

Personal ads were an entirely new form of text to emerge in this period. They established themselves in the mainstream press just as the first novels appeared in bookstores, and this is no coincidence. The two share a number of characteristics. *The Power of Sympathy* (1791) by William Hill Brown, *Charlotte Temple* by Susanna Rowson (1794), and *The Coquette* (1797) by Hannah Webster Foster: their plots all center upon a strikingly similar narrative of a woman who allows herself to be seduced, resulting in her downfall. In literary terms, they demonstrated a newfound focus on the individual, as well as on the pursuit of happiness. They also, like personal ads, provided communities with a shared interest to discuss in the street or at the coffeehouse: "Have you read the bit in Chapter Six where . . . ?" "Did you see the ad in the *Gazette* today?" Both offered a way for a nascent nation to define itself through the power of the pen.

Peter

Philadelphia, 1848

Is this it?

That's what I thought to myself as I lay in bed, staring out the window at the moon peeping through the muslin curtains.

There's got to be more to life, hasn't there? Surely it was ok to hope for more?

I loved being a doctor, I really did, but I needed someone to help me grow the business. To charm patients, then come the evening charm the local great and good: pour them whiskey, play the piano, pretend to lose at whist.

And if she was pretty, too, and liked dogs, and wasn't scared of blood—well, that would be wonderful.

(I didn't even dare to dream she might share the night times with me as well.)

And so, I decided to place an advertisement.

CHAPTER THREE

"TIRED OF THE EVERLASTING SAMENESS OF A BACHELOR'S LIFE": MEN ON THE EAST COAST, C. 1840–1860

P hiladelphia.

June 25, 1841.

The *Public Ledger* (price: one cent) was rolling off the presses.

A number of merchant ships from Kingston, Liverpool, and Londonderry had sailed into port. There was an election coming up for a new sheriff. A letter to the editor complained of the "stench" from the gutter at Ninth and Catherine Streets and there was an article about whether the Reading Railroad Company would still make a profit transporting coal now that it had to compete with the Schuylkill Canal.

Dr. Lee W. Buffington, who ran the dispensary on Fifth Street below Chestnut, was accused of using lunar caustic to burn the shape of a cross onto the forehead of his thirteen-year-old apprentice, Eliza Sharpe, as a punishment for her "singing early in the morning, and also telling falsehoods." And a policeman who went to 33 Almond Street to arrest a man for breaching the peace was startled to find the perpetrator's three children, "one who had just died from the smallpox, and the other two lying upon rags on the floor, afflicted with the same loathsome disease in its worst form," while the mother lay drunk nearby. "The father had decamped."

There was also a detailed account from Washington, DC, of the proceedings of the Twenty-Seventh Congress under President John Tyler. Top of the agenda was the debate over the Bankruptcy Act, America's first bankruptcy law, which was passed later that year.

And then, there were the ads, which were so plentiful and compelling that it is a miracle the rest of this book got written. They tell the story of a metropolis in smudged black ink. There were "For Sale" ads for granite, garden hoses, bonnet trimmings, limes, lumber, clocks, a second-hand steam engine, a makeup for the skin called "vegetable rouge" that "gives to the countenance a bloom impossible on the closest inspection to detect from nature," pets (including birds, guinea pigs, and lap dogs), and parasols "including all styles now in vogue" and "small sized parasols for children." Shopkeepers advertised the arrival of new shipments of tea, coffee, molasses, limes, cocoa, and gunpowder. There was also lots of coal on offer.

Almost a whole page of ads was given over to quack remedies for every ailment imaginable: "female complaints," "bowel complaints," worms, lowness of spirits, measles, asthma, baldness, "all secret diseases" (presumably venereal in nature), and a preparation known as Sand's Remedy for skin diseases such as "Blotched Face, Pimples, Frosted Feet and Barber's Itch" accompanied by the claim that it "never fails to effect the perfect cure." Why not try Gilbert's Family Pills for an astonishingly wide range of complaints, especially as "For Females, these Pills are particularly adapted for removing the distressing headache so prevalent with the Sex, depression of Spirits, dullness of Sight." There were no less than four large ads for Dr. Gourand's depilatory powder "for the removal of superfluous hair," including the "furze on the lip, when annoying, or the short hair on the back of a Lady's neck, when too apparent," $1 a bottle and cheap at the price.

An $8 reward "in hard silver money" was offered for the return of "an indentured apprentice to Chimney Sweeping" described as "a right black boy, named John Cook, aged 15 years. He has big eyes and a down and rogueish look." There were ads for plumbers and attorneys, for a lost red cow "nearly fat," and a dueling pistol; for rooms to rent to single gentlemen or married couples (never to single women), some even with "Hot and Cold baths free." There were scores of job ads, including for two men to shear sheep, a governess, "A girl," some weavers, a hundred laborers to work on the Delaware division of the Pennsylvania canal, and "a leader and eighteen or twenty musicians who play upon wind instruments."

And amid this cacophony of capitalism, there was an ad that began, "Wanted, A Wife."

Public Ledger, *June 25, 1841*

In the fifty years after the Revolution, personal ads remained uncommon, but they did begin to appear in farther-flung locations. I was able to find examples in newspapers in each of the states. Take one of the earliest ones in Georgia:

TO *MATRIMONIAL CANDIDATES.*
Wanted, a WIFE, from fifteen to twenty-five years of age. She must be of a respectable family, liberally educated, inclined to industry so far as to look after domestic affairs, capable of arranging a dinner table in the most modern style, also of entering a drawing or ball room *gracefully*—edifying in conversation, truly chaste, and partial to children. Should the advertiser steer clear of misfortune in his commercial transactions, which are extensive and profitable at present, she will be enabled to appear with the gayest of her sex; and, in every respect, her pleasure and happiness will be her guardian's study. Any young lady considering herself possessed of the above accomplishments, will be punctually attended with the greatest secrecy, by addressing to "T. T." at the *Savannah Republican office.*

Savannah Republican, *July 21, 1818*

I found comparable examples everywhere from Pennsylvania ("with about $2,000 as a patrimony, sweet temper, spend little, be a good housewife, and born in America"—1824) to Washington, DC ("she shall prefer historical, geographical and biographical reading to light and frivolous novels"—1827) to Virginia ("must be fully competent to take charge of all household matters, and the more particularly the well management of servants, as nothing is more disagreeable to the subscriber than complaints of their worthlessness and powers of teasing"—1838).

In 1834, a personal ad appeared in William Lloyd Garrison's abolitionist newspaper *The Liberator* from "a friend of equal rights" who was "convinced that it would be his duty, and it is his determination, to bear testimony against prejudice by marrying a Colored Woman . . . Information would be thankfully received of any young, respectable, and intelligent Colored Woman, (entirely or chiefly of African descent), who would be willing to endure the insults and reproaches that would be heaped upon her for being the partner of a white man . . ." Opinion-formers around the country debated the merits of this approach. A North Carolina newspaper printed an editorial deploring the ad, calling it the result of "the fanaticism and folly" of the abolitionist movement, which in the 1830s was gaining increasing support, especially from free African Americans in the north and from women.

The first newspaper regularly to feature personal ads was Philadelphia's biggest seller, the *Public Ledger*. Founded in 1836 by two printers from New York, William Swain and Arunah S. Abell, the *Ledger* was an innovator in its field.

In the early days, Philadelphia's newspapers were priced at five or six cents a copy. With a combined circulation of about 8,000 copies, they were bought mainly by the well-off or by coffeehouses or taverns. The *Ledger* was the first newspaper in the city to drop its price to just one penny, following a national trend known as "the penny press." Instead of making a profit from the cover price, these papers funded themselves from advertising. For the *Ledger*, this radical financial decision proved an immediate success: its circulation increased to 15,000 by 1840 and 40,000 by 1850.

Newspapers' low prices attracted a different class of readership with new expectations, which included lively ads. An ad in the *Ledger* cost fifty cents, except for marriage and funeral notices, which cost twenty-five. As editor, Swain had experimented with "runaway wife" ads—that is, ads trying to sever ties with a wife, rather than gain one. For example, in 1836, John G. Alben of South Street used the *Ledger* to announce to his fellow Philadelphians that "My wife Sarah, at the instigation of her devilish mother and her not any better sisters, having left my bed and board, I hereby caution any person or persons against trusting the said Sarah on my account, as I will not pay any debts contracted by her from this date." These sorts of "runaway wife" ads have, strangely, received considerable attention from historians in a way that personal ads have not.

There were frequently news stories next to the "runaway wife" ads about wives who had run off or been beaten or even murdered. One might wonder why a woman would want to get married in the first place, or even take the risk of responding to the ad of a man who was a complete stranger to them. But what choice did they have? While Philadelphia had more opportunities than most cities for women's economic independence, these were still limited; rooms or boarding houses advertised only to single men or married couples. Most women therefore had little choice but to hitch their lot to a man.

In 1840, an editorial appeared in the *Ledger* that, while surely written to increase its sales of personal ads, now seems decades, even centuries, ahead of its time. "Advertising for wives," it argued, "is becoming every day more and more usual, and is viewed with less and less prejudice. The plain truth is that there is no better mode to procure a good partner . . . False delicacy is a great stumbling block to human happiness . . ." It cites a man from the South who successfully advertised for a wife, going on to claim that most ads received on average between 25 and 500 replies.

The editorial claimed that the extensive geographical reach of personal ads contributed to their appeal among those considering placing one. "Say, for instance, that an advertisement of this kind should appear in the *Ledger*; there it will soon meet the observation of every respectable lady in the city, in the Northern Liberties, Southwark, Kensington, Camden, Germantown, and fifty other towns and villages and rural locations in a circle of fifty miles radius. . . . More female loveliness and perfection than you ever dreamed of will expand before you, like a parterre of the most exquisite flowers waiting invitingly to be plucked." It concludes, "Oh, bachelor, if thou art human, think of this and hesitate no longer."

Throughout the 1840s, 1850s, and 1860s, there were almost always a couple of ads a day in the *Ledger*. It pioneered the genre.

I spent weeks trawling through every edition of the paper, and I could see the development of a standard lexicon in personal ads. They were invariably written in the third person, which allowed the author to distance himself from the text and present it as if it were news: "Stop press! Man wants wife!" as it were. Certain phrases recur—"Discretion assured," "Letters post paid"—but the language tends to be straightforward, with no acronyms or abbreviations and also little creativity or wit.

Who were these men who decided to confide in readers of the *Ledger* that they were "tired of the everlasting sameness of a Bachelor's life," as one put it? Most are in their twenties, although there is the occasional outlier, such as the "widower, aged 61." A typical description is something along the lines of "a modest young man, 23 years of age, (of most unexceptional character), and good prospects" or "a respectable young Gentleman, well established in a lucrative business." Others are even more blatant in this regard, for example using the phrase "in easy pecuniary circumstances." By putting their economic status front and center, they signal how important this was to the marriage contract.

"Of good character" is the attribute that appears most often. "Respectable" is also popular. Others are more specific, for example: "good looking, well educated," "healthy, moral, genteel, intelligent; does not drink, chew or smoke," or "in good health and temper, not very ugly." On display was a new form of textual courtship where the focus was on the attributes of the man, rather than the woman, in contrast to courtly poetry where it tends to be the other way around.

Background information is rare, but pops up occasionally: there is one advertiser "from one of the Southeaster States" whose father is "a large and respectable" plantation owner, "A Native of Germany," "A Yankee widower," "lately returned from India," "a resident of the country," and "a writer."

The ads reveal what a single young man living in Philadelphia in the 1840s wanted in a wife.

Easily the top priority was being aged between eighteen and twenty-five—the years when a woman is biologically most fertile. The most desired personality traits were being "amiable," "agreeable," or "of good disposition." Academic studies of human courtship have found that social skills of this sort have always been of paramount importance in mate choice, perhaps because they suggest an ability to sustain a relationship even in the face of significant challenges.

Also on display was a high degree of class consciousness. The men wanted "a young lady of Refinement" or one who was "respectably connected." "Easy" or "engaging" manners were in high demand and the perfect candidate would also have a "good education" or, even better, a "good English education."

Domesticity was a concern, too: these men sought a woman who was "economical," "understands or is willing to learn housekeeping," "a knowledge of housewifery," or "of industrious habits." "Good health" and "strict religious habits" also recur.

Interests or accomplishments are mentioned in a way that would have been unheard-of a century before: "has some taste for literature and music," "accomplishments in music preferred," "should by all means be able to sing 'Home, Sweet Home' and 'Share My Cottage,' but must not allow her voice to reach as high as 'Marble Halls.'" This reflected the changing role of the middle-class wife: socially ambitious men no longer wanted a coworker so much as an adornment to show off at parties.

Physical appearance seems not to have been a top priority, or at least not one many were prepared to admit in the pages of a newspaper. References were vague: "Good-looking," "Well-looking," "Medium size," "Some beauty required."

A few were explicit about the financial realities of marriage: "an amiable, economical and wealthy Lady, upon whom he will fix a dower from $2,000 to $10,000," "must have money," "a small competency desirable," "have some property," or "a few thousands." Others went out of their way to state that this was not about money: "Money is no object to the applicant, as he has made out to save some few dollars during his bachelor life."

But why did these men choose to advertise for a wife rather than meeting one the old-fashioned way, through family, friends, or neighbors?

The short answer is: Philadelphia's population explosion.

Once upon a time, everyone in Philadelphia knew each other's business: who had just moved in next door, the name of the new vicar's daughter across the street. No longer. What had been a mercantile city of about 30,000 people during the Revolution had, by 1850, grown into the nation's first major industrial metropolis with a population of more than 120,000 people. The agrarian society of the previous decades was replaced by a fast-growing capitalist, commercial society. Its success was due in large part to its proximity to the Pennsylvanian coalfields, which contained an astonishing 75 percent of the world's anthracite coal. Barges delivered this natural resource up the Schuylkill River, where it took over from wood stoves and water wheels in providing the huge amounts of power required to keep the city's factories running day and night.

You could easily go a whole day using only products manufactured in Philadelphia: soap to wash in, sugar for your tea, paper to write a letter, paint for your walls, the steel in the knife you used to cut cheese, leather for your shoes, lace for your bonnet, fertilizers for your horse's paddock, the malt liquor you drank in a nearby tavern, the printed book you read in bed at night, the iron candle holder you blew out before you went to sleep. If only the factories could manufacture you a wife.

Perhaps lovelorn bankers placed some of the ads. Philadelphia was the home of the first commercial bank, the first national bank, and the first savings banks, as well as the first U.S. Mint and stock exchange. It was also a pioneer of the insurance industry: brokers clustered around the wharves ready to pounce on merchant ships. Philadelphia boasted the world's first penitentiary, lending library, and municipal water system, as well as the country's first hospital, suspension bridge, and zoo. The thing was, though, that libraries and hospitals were all very well, but unless you were a bookworm or a nurse fetishist, they were unlikely to help a single gent find a lady friend.

Many of the mechanisms that had previously underpinned society, including but not limited to the realm of matchmaking, now proved inadequate for those working long hours in a factory or office without a community of long-standing friends or family around to help them search for a suitable life partner. There were also fewer nosy neighbors or interfering relatives around to scrutinize and criticize one's behavior. This freed people to look for love in whatever way they chose.

A significant number of the men who advertise explain that they are "a stranger in the city." Philadelphia was a huge draw for those in search of riches. Tens of thousands of young, rural folk flocked there in search of new opportunities, due not only to its prosperity but also to its accessibility: America's earliest hard-surfaced road, which opened in 1794, was sixty-six miles long between Philadelphia and Lancaster, while 1832 brought the city's first railroad, heading north to Germantown.

It is also possible that the "stranger in the city" was an immigrant from abroad. Between 1847 and 1854, over 120,000 immigrants arrived in Philadelphia, making it the nation's fourth most popular immigrant destination. Three out of ten Philadelphians were foreign born, mostly German and Irish, and therefore lacked the long-standing community ties—family, friends, neighbors—that would once have helped snag a spouse.

A number of Philadelphians admitted in their ads that they worked too hard to have time to meet women. As one put it, "The business of the advertiser has occupied his whole attention, and has left him but little time to cultivate the accomplishments which mark the fashionable man of the present day; but in lieu of them he offers an honest and confiding heart." One "young man of business habits" was explicit about his belief that, for a time-poor businessman, personal ads made the matchmaking process more efficient, declaring in 1844 that he was "desirous of uniting himself to a young lady of good education and family, possessed of a moderate competency. Her age should not exceed twenty-five." He explained that "Being closely confined by his business, he cannot devote the time necessary to a protracted courtship; he therefore avails himself of the medium of a publication to express his wishes."

The period's restrictive social etiquette didn't help. Opportunities for middle-class men and women to meet and mingle were limited. Most Philadelphians lived in single-family townhouses or single-sex boarding houses, and places of employment were similarly divided. Respectable women were discouraged from entering most public spaces, so while you might meet during a stroll in the park or at a bookseller's, starting up a conversation was difficult. If you came across a woman in a tavern or even at the theatre, you might worry she was a prostitute. Church was one of the few times the sexes coexisted outside of the home, but fewer people than before attended regularly and, even then, they did not necessarily feel the need to worship in the same place every time. No wonder many advertisers bemoaned their "limited female acquaintance."

The most common explanation given by Philadelphians for advertising for love, though, was shyness. "His extreme modesty prevents him from addressing directly any young lady," lamented one; another revealed he is, "Of rather a bashful, retiring disposition, which has hitherto prevented him from mixing much in female society." Shyness, it turns out, is not a recent invention.

Shyness, or "extreme modesty and diffidence," as one advertiser put it, is also an entirely valid response to the potentially horrifying prospect of talking to someone you don't know, especially someone of the opposite sex. An ad in a newspaper allowed one to circumvent the embarrassment of trying to figure out who was in the market for marriage and who was not. Those interested were asked to send a letter to their prospective paramour care of either the Philadelphia Post Office or the offices of the *Ledger* at Third and Chestnut Streets, a busy thoroughfare in the middle of downtown. In this way a face-to-face meeting was postponed until both parties got to know each other a little via pen and paper.

The geographical reach of Philadelphia's newspapers made them especially effective at disseminating the ads. Newly built canals, railroads, and roads meant relatively easy access to the western regions, a major source of men and women. Other areas of Pennsylvania soon caught on, too. In 1853, the *Blairsville Apalachian* [sic], a short-lived newspaper near Pittsburgh, featured an ad for a wife willing to "reside in a country town in the western part of Pennsylvania, and worth not less than $5,000."

A WIFE WANTED.

A YOUNG LADY between 20 and 25 years of age, medium size, good character, willing to reside in a country town in the western part of Pennsylvania, and worth not less than $5,000, will hear of an opportunity to get married to a gentleman of good character, in a respectable profession, but without money (having spent all he had in obtaining his profession) by addressing (post paid) "ANTONIO," Apalachian office, Blairsville, Indiana county, Pa. References given and required.

Blairsville Apalachian, *February 2, 1853*

The *Pittsburgh Daily Post* commented snootily in response, "All that we have to say is that ladies in possession of fortunes of $5,000 are not very apt to bestow their affections upon seedy professional gentlemen." This seems a bit harsh. Other rural Pennsylvanians were more down-to-earth in their requirements, as in the case of "WHW" who described himself as "strictly moral and religious in all his habits" and who, on Christmas Eve, 1861, offered readers of the *Lewisburg Chronicle* a modest rundown of what he wanted in a wife: "She must write a good hand, bake a good loaf of bread, and be able to get as good a dinner as can be scared up in three counties."

Personal ads reached Baltimore, Ohio, in the early 1850s: its population stood at about 170,000, up 65 percent from a decade earlier, making it the nation's second most populous city after New York. One of the earliest ads, in the *Baltimore Sun*, was from "a gentleman of ample fortune and prepossessing appearance" looking for "a lady of useful accomplishments, and of an affectionate disposition, between the age of 18 and 25 years."

Baltimore Sun, *August 3, 1853*

Cincinnati, Ohio, which was the first industrial city west of the Appalachians, was not far behind, with the *Cincinnati Daily Press* featuring a personal ad almost every day from the late 1850s onward.

Many ads continued to appear in New England, too, and it was no longer just gentlemen who advertised. In 1849, a twenty-five-year-old New Jersey mechanic "in middling circumstances" publicized his want of a wife, while in 1860 there was an ad from a forty-year-old Massachusetts farmer named Peter Cowles, who lived with his five children and his older brother. Peter had given a lot of thought to what he wanted in a wife: "dark flowing hair, a little mite curly, dimples on her cheeks, mild, gentle, slow, with pleasant eyes looking out of her head. I don't want a glass-eyed or lantern-jawed woman, one that is as cross as blazes and gads about, gossiping and making mischief all over town." He does not sound like much of a catch, but perhaps some woman somewhere decided to settle for him nonetheless.

Ads soon spread south through the East Coast. In 1859, the local paper in New Bern, at the time the largest city in North Carolina, featured an ad from a "young gentleman of this town, having an education and a small competency, and of domestic habits" searching for a woman with "a good education, an even temper, and some personal property in possession."

Daily Delta, *July 19, 1859*

South Carolina was not far behind. In the *Intelligencer* in 1861, there appeared an ad from a gentleman "anxious to retire from 'bachelor' ranks" with a very specific idea of what he wanted in a wife: "Weight, between 100 and 135 pounds; height, between five feet and five feet six inches; teeth regular, perfect and genuine, without exception; black hair and eyes preferred, though blue eyes and auburn hair might be acceptable. A good English education is necessary. Wealth is not required, but those possessing it will state the amount. A good supply of temper is very much admired."

The growth of personal ads led to the first rumblings of moral outrage against them. An editorial in the *Boston Post* in 1854 spluttered that there were "few things more amusing in newspapers than the incongruous mixture of business and sentiment, love and lucre, innocence and impudence, which form the staple of 'matrimonial' ads." It goes on to quote an ad from a "young gentleman" seeking "a matrimonial alliance with a young lady not over sixteen years of age. She must be pretty, well developed, and of undoubted respectability." The newspaper comments: "The particular point of 'development' is not specified; he may allude to the bust (that she may not die prematurely of consumption), probably not to the ancle, and certainly not to the brain—any young lady who has the good fortune to be 'well developed' in that region not being likely to be caught by a matrimonial ad." So that told him.

Snark from a columnist was not going to make personal ads go away, though. They were a direct response to the fact that, between 1820 and 1860, the urban population of the United States increased by an astonishing 797 percent. One in every six Americans lived in a city. Cities like Philadelphia, Baltimore, and Cincinnati became so huge and impersonal that word-of-mouth was no longer a sufficient matchmaking technique. Newspaper editors leapt in to fill the gap. The newspaper replaced the marketplace as the principal public forum where people shared information, made connections, and formed alliances. Thus, the existence of personal ads reveals the way that urbanization creates profound shifts in the way a society functions. Advertising for love became an essential element of any urbanized society—like a postal service or a sewer system, but sexier.

Mary

Washington, DC, 1860

I loved the pastor, you see. My whole life.

And then he went and married my sister. Well, I thought I was going to die of grief.

My mother felt there was no rush for me to get married as well, but she was wrong.

I didn't have the language to explain why. Suffice it to say that every time I woke up in the night drenched in sweat, I knew I needed to lie with a man to help relieve the suffering.

I couldn't tell anyone, of course.

Then, one gray day when I was listlessly skimming the newspaper for governess jobs, I came across an advertisement for a "Husband Wanted."

What a splendid idea!

Perhaps my options were not limited after all to the belligerent widower over the road, the lecherous bank clerk with whom I deposited the rent our lodgers paid mother every week, or the brother of my school friend Susanna who was lovely but who coughed up blood every time he tried to speak to me and by all accounts would be dead within a year.

And so, I decided to place an advertisement.

CHAPTER FOUR

"Someone to Share My Sweets or My Bitters, Whichever Our Lot May Be": Women on the East Coast, c. 1840–1860

Husband Wanted. A young lady of twenty-five, availing herself of the privilege which the present year gives to her sex, hereby makes it known her want to all respectable single gentlemen. She has neither wealth nor beauty to recommend her, but possesses a goodly share of those qualities which Solomon recommended young men to seek in a companion for life. No fop with kid gloves, gold rings, an eyeglass, and a pocket full of musk need present himself, as the young lady much prefers brains to any of those killing qualifications. Good recommendations are required.

Angeline Hopewell had received just one proposal of marriage in her life. She had turned it down because the gentleman in question had a severe squint, which she feared would be passed on to their children.

On the last day of September 1855, Angeline stood in front of her bedroom mirror and said to herself, "Tomorrow I shall be twenty-nine—twenty-nine! Who would have believed it?" She "had plodded life's weary pilgrimage alone, and [. . .] was now resolved to do so no longer." With this in mind, she made a dramatic decision: "tomorrow I am going to improve the privilege allotted to my sex, and I intend to persevere until I succeed in the accomplishment of my purpose." She desperately hoped to avoid "the obloquy always cast upon old maids . . ."

The following year, 1856, was a leap year, when tradition held that women could propose to men rather than always vice versa. In Angeline's mind, "if I do not improve the present opportunity, I shall be so old before another leap year that no one will want me, for a woman changes fast after she passes thirty."

And so, on New Year's Day, Angeline put an ad in the local newspaper under the headline "Husband Wanted."

It "created a great sensation among the masculines" and received plenty of replies, including one from a Simon Goodwell, a wealthy merchant and the widowed father of two young children. The day they met, Angeline liked him so much that she immediately paid a call to the family of his late wife, who were happy to vouch for him. They were married by the end of the week.

The moral of the story? "Girls, old maids, old widows, don't lie down and despair, but pluck up courage, go and do likewise."

Or so Miss Harriet Graves imagined how Angeline's future might play out in a short story she wrote for Pennsylvania's *Pittston Gazette* in 1856. Years later, Graves would get a job transcribing Emily Dickinson's poems after her death. For now, though, she was too busy writing what was essentially propaganda for advertising for love, a genre to which mid-19th century women were increasingly drawn.

⊗

For most women, a husband was the only route to financial security. As Jane Austen put it, "single women have a dreadful propensity for being poor—which is one very strong argument in favour of Matrimony." The alternative was destitution, prostitution, or throwing oneself on the mercy of generous relatives.

A husband was also a means of escape from parental control toward a life of one's own. What else were young, middle-class, single women supposed to do with their time, other than die of boredom? There were few employment opportunities, female secondary education was rare, and American women were not admitted to college until 1837, when Oberlin College allowed them through its doors. Many faced the prospect of years and years when society considered them no longer a child but also not yet, in the parlance of the day, "settled." During that period they were expected to make themselves useful around the house until they snagged a man. Contemporary diaries record an endless social whirl of house calls; goodness, it must have been dull.

And if a suitable candidate for marriage had not presented himself by the ripe old age of, say, twenty-two, what then?

"Husband Wanted" ads were not common in the mid-19th century, but there were far more of them than you might expect, and they are hugely revealing about the duality between the public and private faces of women in this period. Women rarely kept diaries or wrote memoirs, so the ads they placed constitute precious evidence of their voices. These women were not the norm, but rather the very boldest and most empowered of their sex. Instead of passively waiting for a man, any man, to show an interest, they made a decision to circumvent social convention and become active players in their own life choices.

The first "Husband Wanted" ads, like the first "Wife Wanted" ads, were satirical in intent. One of the earliest appeared in the *Alexandria Gazette* in Washington, DC, just before Christmas 1818. It was purportedly from "two young ladies [who] wish to make it known for the edification of those young men who are votaries to Hymen that they are perfectly acquainted with the theory of making puddings, apple dumplings, and other delicacies—an accomplishment which is not the smallest source of domestic felicity." One of them was looking for a man who was "adept in the art of sowing potatoes, planting beans, etc.," while the other prioritized a "head well stored with small talk (good sense not requisite), and no questions asked on important subjects."

The intention here was to mock the ways single women tried to sell themselves to single men, for example by highlighting the tastiness of their apple dumplings, reflecting a widespread concern that women had become too blatant and indelicate in their efforts to attract a husband.

But what choice did they have?

The always-innovative *Public Ledger* in Philadelphia, still under the editorship of William Swain, was the first newspaper in the nation to regularly feature "Husband Wanted" ads. It was a small but significant victory in the fight for women to have an equal voice to men.

It was a Tuesday in May 1840 and the front page carried a philosophical essay entitled "Does A Fish Think?" and a report from the first session of the 26th Congress. There had been a debate about a bill designed to reduce tax fraud: "Mr Adams was armed literally from head to foot with information," it insisted, revealing that the incorrect use of the word "literally" is by no means a new problem.

There was also local news, including a long piece about a dispute between the council and the Rothschilds in London about a loan, a story about the City Council installing an additional street lamp and repaving various streets, and an account of a lawyer who was arrested at the theatre for disorderly conduct but was then freed by a judge because "it was clear he was labouring at the time under a temporary derangement, caused remotely by peculiarly affecting and harrowing circumstances."

Then there were the numerous ads. They included a "Missing Person" ad for a man who had "strayed from the Asylum for the Insane," Lost (a large black-and-white Newfoundland dog called Tom King) and Found (a purse on Sixth Street), and an announcement about a meeting of the Temperance Society at 2:00 P.M. followed by the Female Temperance Society at 3:00 P.M. There were goods for sale, including "a lot of Fancy Pigeons, comprising Groppers, Carriers, and Fantails," as well as an extraordinary array of quack medicines, such as a syrup designed to banish "the peculiar lethargic feelings and dizziness so common in the Spring."

Lurking among them was one of the earliest genuine ads from a woman looking for a husband.

The advertiser, "S.J.K.," "desirous of changing single blessedness for matrimony," describes herself as "A few years above the teens." Women in this period wed at an average age of just twenty-two, so there is an implicit concern here about ending up a spinster (which was originally a term for a woman who spun yarn, but gradually acquired negative connotations for any unmarried female).

Public Ledger, May 12, 1840

In terms of physical appearance, "S.J.K." says she has "good teeth, full face, good complexion." Each attribute is an indicator of general healthiness and by association fertility, and therefore an important selling point, especially to those steeped in the contemporary literature of American health reformers such as Orson Squire Fowler, who argued for the importance of "pedigree" when choosing a breeding partner. In his view, what mattered was not wealth or status, but a sound physical constitution and ancestors who had lived into old age.

And her accomplishments? She was "acquainted with music, endowed with vocal powers." In this way she asserts her gentility, along with the surprising claim that she lives "in her own house." This was rare for a single woman in this period, but emphasizes that this advertiser was in many ways atypical of her sex.

"S.J.K." was looking for a husband who was "not beyond middle age"—that is, not too old, perhaps because she wanted children and hence high-quality sperm. It was important to her that he was "perfectly sober" and "an American"— presumably meaning born in America, a complex assertion, revealing a prejudice against first generation immigrants that was to poison the nation's public discourse for many years to come. Finally, she demands "evidence of sincerity of the applicant." She was savvy enough to comprehend that ads of this sort were ripe for exploitation by jokesters and fraudsters.

The newspaper lays bare the severely limited options available to women, trapped as they were in the grip of society's absurd double standards. The *Ledger* that day also carried an ad from one Edmund McDonald who sought to absolve himself from paying his wife Susan's debts now that she had left him; an account of a servant named Mary Balentine who stole bank notes from her employer Joseph Ashton which she then swallowed in a panic when arrested, and was sentenced to eighteen (eighteen!) months in prison; and a long piece about the celebrated Austrian ballerina Fanny Elssler, who had recently embarked on a tour of America. While in New York she had been linked to John Van Buren, son of President Martin Van Buren; she then headed to Philadelphia, where the *Ledger* was deeply unimpressed with her act ("A flea can skip nine hundred and ninety-nine times higher") and criticized her for the high price of the tickets, implying that it was unseemly for a woman to earn so much money.

The *Public Ledger* continued to publish "Husband Wanted" ads throughout the 1840s and 1850s.

Public Ledger, *November 5, 1845*

Public Ledger, *December 4, 1850*

Public Ledger, *March 16, 1852*

These women gave away little about their own personal qualities or circumstances; the most we get, in 1845, is one who describes herself as "respectably connected, has been well educated, has some few accomplishments, and all the sterling qualities calculated to make home happy."

They are very clear, however, about what they are looking for in a potential partner. Age-wise, he should be around forty. One is specifically after an "American Mechanic," intriguingly; maybe she was having problems with her machinery. Qualities mentioned most frequently include "respectable," "honest," "amiable," and "educated," as well as "industrious" and "generous," thereby indicating that financial stability was (understandably) important to them.

For many, "sobriety" was a top priority. Excessive drinking among Philadelphian men was widespread. On average, those over fifteen consumed nearly seven gallons of pure alcohol a year—three times as much as is drunk today. This wreaked havoc on the lives of families everywhere. The anti-alcohol movement—which had grown out of a general fervor for reform that swept the nation starting in the 1830s and in 1851 won its first statewide legislative victory when Maine passed a law banning its sale—was especially active in Philadelphia. Ads for the Temperance Society were often to be found just a few columns over from ads for "Husbands Wanted." While today it would be rare to specify "perfectly sober" and would reek of less-than-ideal past relationships, back then it simply showed a realistic appraisal of the playing field.

Some of the women asked interested parties to leave a note at the newspaper's offices, but many instead asked them to write care of Blood's Despatch. Founded in 1842 by Daniel Otis Blood and his brother Walter, Blood's Despatch was the most successful of Philadelphia's private mail companies and issued the world's first pictorial stamp. It was based on South Sixth Street above Chestnut, just a block away from the Liberty Bell and Independence Hall—which seems fitting, when for many women liberty and independence was exactly what they hoped to achieve through their personal ad.

There were a number of social and economic reasons why these "Husband Wanted" ads began to appear so frequently in Philadelphia's newspapers in the 1840s.

In the decades after the Revolution, expanding trade throughout the states generated significant wealth in commercial centers like Philadelphia, resulting in a consumption-oriented lifestyle of the wives, sisters, and daughters of these merchants. Household inventories of the period reveal all the clutter associated with a genteel existence: teacups, napkins, silverware, as well as a significant amount of household help. No longer forced to labor all day planting crops or washing clothes, middle-class women suddenly had the luxury of time on their hands to sit around and chat, sew, read novels, drink tea, or shop for clothes, hats, or even husbands by dreaming up fanciful schemes like writing personal ads.

These women were not only wealthier than ever before, but also more literate. In the first half of the 19th century, it became standard practice to teach girls to read and write, the better to prepare them to be mothers to the next generation of active American citizens. By 1850, the majority of white women were literate, whereas a hundred years earlier about half could not even sign their own name. Some even became published authors, such as the novelists Harriet Beecher Stowe and Catharine Sedgwick.

American women also enjoyed a great deal of freedom compared to their European counterparts. According to Alexis de Tocqueville in *Democracy in America* (1840):

> Nowhere are young women surrendered so early or completely to their own guidance. Long before an American girl arrives at the age of marriage, her emancipation from maternal control begins; she has scarcely ceased to be a child when she already thinks for herself, speaks with freedom, and acts on her own impulse. . . . [E]ven

amidst the independence of early youth, an American woman is always mistress of herself.

Writing and placing a personal ad was therefore not too tricky, at least in terms of logistics.

In 1848, the first women's rights convention was held in Seneca Falls; the same year, New York passed the first Married Woman's Property Act. One result was that women everywhere felt a little more empowered to forge their own path and, in the years that immediately followed, there was a surge in ads from women all over the states. Take, for example, "Ada" in Alexandria, Virginia, in 1851:

> My husband must be from twenty to thirty; good sense preferred to good looks; and no simpering fool, who imagines a lady taken off her feet by his smiles, no uneducated ape in lavender kids and yellow stick, no mature dandy, such as promenade for smiles of silly girls and impudent stares, no mustached baboon, need apply, as no one will please me but a sensible, educated gentleman who appreciates domestic happiness by the possession of one heart.

Up to this point, most female advertisers had chosen to edge themselves and their own needs and desires out of the picture. Not Ada.

Comfortably well-off women like Ada could increasingly decide whom they wanted to marry. In 1847, the Argentine writer Domingo Sarmiento commented that, in America, "The unmarried woman . . . is as free as a butterfly until marriage. She travels alone, wanders about the streets of the city, carries on several chaste and public love affairs under the indifferent eyes of her parents, receives visits from persons who have not been presented to her family, and returns home from a dance at two o'clock in the morning accompanied by the young man with whom she has waltzed or polkaed exclusively all night." The control parents exerted over their adult children was diminishing as the children married later and asserted their independence.

Ideas about what made a great marriage were also changing. Writer Judith Sargent Murray knew a couple in Philadelphia who, in her view, had the ideal relationship: they lived in "perfect equality. . . as two friends, unusually well matched in understanding, taste, and knowledge." Anyone who has been in a long-term romantic relationship knows that the likelihood that these two people really lived in "perfect equality" is slim, but never mind. Even to aspire to this was revolutionary.

A companionate marriage was increasingly held up as the goal. As Mary Orne Tucker rhapsodized, "Souls must be kindred to make the bands silken, all other I call unions of hands, not hearts,—I rejoice that the knot which binds me was not tied with any mercenary feelings, and that my heart is under the same sweet subjection as my hand." Studies of life in New England in the first half of the 19th century reveal that descriptions of what people wanted in a life partner began to include compatibility and companionship, along with thrift and diligence. "Husband Wanted" ads of the period confirm this. They do not mention companionship specifically, but instead employ terms like "amiable," "personably agreeable," or "a good disposition."

An ad in the *Public Ledger* on November 5, 1845, called for a husband "capable of making a wife happy." This marks the first time being "happy" was openly upheld as a marital goal. Fifty years after the Declaration of Independence, when the Founding Fathers declared the pursuit of happiness a human right, it was also coming to be viewed as a wife's right.

Novels of the period further encouraged the ideal of marrying for love. "I have always said I would never marry a man that I was not willing to die for," remarked the heroine in Catharine Sedgwick's *Clarence* (1830). A pioneering novel of manners about a young woman searching for a husband in New York City, *Clarence* was a huge bestseller, contributing significantly to the development of the first distinctively American body of literature and transforming Sedgwick into the nation's most successful woman writer. A native of Massachusetts, she herself turned down a number of marriage proposals, making the decision instead to remain single and devote her life to her work, confiding in her niece that "so many I have loved have made a shipwreck of happiness in marriage or have found it a dreary joyless condition." Nonetheless, her books cast marriage as the goal of every young woman; in her final novel, *Married or Single?* (1857), she does debate the issue, but comes down on the side of matrimony.

Highly literate, with time on their hands, middle-class women were the nation's first mass book buyers. In the pre–Civil War era, *Harper's* magazine estimated that 80 percent of the reading public was female. It is all but certain that among them was one Kate Darsie of Westmoreland County, Pennsylvania.

The year 1860 was a leap year, and Kate Darsie was in the mood for love: "As it has become fashionable in the Eastern as well as the Western cities for young ladies as well as gentlemen to make known their wants through the columns of a public journal, and as this is the year when ladies can make free to do so," Kate explained, she had decided to place a marriage ad in one of Philadelphia's biggest newspapers.

Kate described herself as "five feet; dark hair and eyes, and rather prepossessing in appearance . . . I am not what the world calls rich, but what I prize more highly than gold: a character without a stain."

She sought a husband who "can share my sweets or my bitters, which ever our lot may be, with cheerfulness and a good will." More specifically, her only real stipulation was that "he shall bear an unimpeachable record"—in other words, that he be respectable. In the strict social climate of pre–Civil War Pennsylvania, this quality was prized above all.

Kate's whimsical style of language, and her romantic vision of her and her future husband's life together, which is much closer in tone to a modern ad than a 19th-century one, suggests a woman who has spent a lot of time immersed in romantic novels. Perhaps she had even drawn direct inspiration from Harriet Graves's story eight years earlier in Pennsylvania's *Pittston Gazette*, in which the protagonist puts her faith in the opportunities offered by a leap year.

Kate Darsie never married and almost immediately disappeared from public view, apart from the occasional mention in a Pennsylvanian newspaper when she hosted a card game or volunteered at a charity event. It is frustrating not to know what happened to her; it is a little like one of Catharine Sedgwick's novels, but with the last few pages torn out. But perhaps it is fitting that this is how her story ends: romantic, mysterious, intriguing.

Esther

South Carolina, 1863

One day, I woke up and thought I might die of boredom.

This wasn't a turn of phrase. I actually thought I might die, a victim of the whirl of parties and dress-fittings and small talk and piano lessons. Would I be the first? At least then I'd have done something memorable with my life.

My brothers were so lucky they got to fight the damned Yankees.

I just sat at home waiting for someone to marry me.

Well, one day I decided I'd had enough.

I got Billy, the groom, to saddle up my horse and rode into town to the newspaper office. Just to have a look, you know.

And then I thought to myself: frankly, what do I have to lose?

And so, I decided to place an advertisement.

CHAPTER FIVE

"His Drooping Spirits": The Civil War, 1861–1865

Edwin L. Lybarger lay stretched on his hospital bed in Paducah, Kentucky. He felt he could bear the torturous pain in his leg if only he had something to occupy his thoughts, and reached for the newspaper, which lay forlornly on his bedside table. Perhaps that would give him some ideas.

Edwin had enlisted in a company of volunteer soldiers at Camp Andrews in Mount Vernon, Ohio, as soon as the first shot of the Civil War was fired.

He became a lieutenant in the 43rd Ohio Volunteer Infantry, but during fierce skirmishes at the Battle of Corinth in Mississippi on October 4, 1862, a Confederate bullet smashed into his knee and took him out of action. The stoicism with which he later wrote about the day in his diary is quite something: "The engagement commenced at 4 in the morning. Was wounded about 11 A.M. and left the field. Repulsed the enemy."

Edwin spent the next three months in the hospital, working to regain the use of his leg. During this period, he hit upon the idea of placing a personal ad.

By now, personal ads had become a familiar sight to anyone who regularly read a newspaper, not only on the East Coast and the frontier but increasingly in the South as well. From "Lorenzo" in 1840 in Louisiana's *Daily Picayune* ("in want of a wife . . . must be sober, industrious and neat") to "Echo" in

Florida's *Pensacola Gazette* in 1852 ("Husband Wanted . . . no snuff-taker or tobacco chewer. . . must understand the uses of the quill and the fist, as there will be a good deal of writing and boxing to do"), as well as ads in neighboring states like Arkansas and Alabama, this method of matchmaking was a nation-wide phenomenon by the time the Civil War broke out.

Edwin L. Lybarger

Edwin's ad appeared in a number of local newspapers in Ohio and Kentucky around the time of the Battle of Gettysburg in 1863. It opened not with the words "Wife Wanted" or "Object Matrimony," but instead "Wanted— Correspondent," a phrase that had acquired new meaning during the Civil War.

Letter-writing was widely viewed as a gender-specific form of war work. An article in the *Atlantic Monthly* urged Northern women to give up sewing socks for soldiers: "stitching does not crush rebellion." Instead, they should pick up a pen "with passionate purpose" and channel their "soul of fire" in the form of cheering missives to the front lines. "Follow the soldier to the battlefield with your spirit," it went on. "The great army of letters that marches southward with every morning sun is a powerful engine of war."

Personal ads thus came to fulfill a new function in the early 1860s. To place one was a way for a lonely young man, miles from home and fearful for his life, to seek comfort, as well perhaps to obtain a reminder of home, family, community—in other words, what it was he was fighting for. No doubt the prospect of imminent death also made many worry less about the social stigma (carpe diem and all that). Meanwhile, to reply to one was viewed by respectable society not, as in years gone by, as a shocking moment of folly, but as an act of profound patriotism.

Personal ads placed by both Northern and Southern soldiers were published in a variety of newspapers throughout the war. A significant number came from Fort Monroe, a military encampment on the southern tip of the Virginia Peninsula that remained under Union control throughout the war and became a well-known refuge for escaped slaves. It was also a transfer point for mail exchange, meaning that letters sent from Confederate states to Union states went there first, where they were opened and inspected before being forwarded on. As a result, there is the "young soldier" who "wishes to correspond with some young lady to relieve the tedium of camp life," as well as the "officer, who is suffering from a wound, and has recently been released from Richmond, is desirous of forming a correspondence with some lady for the purpose of cheering his drooping spirit," as he explained in his ad in the *New York Herald* in 1862. Both effectively appeal to female readers' sense of patriotic responsibility.

Others wanted more than just a few scribbled letters; they wanted a wife and kids. The average age of Union soldiers at enlistment was 25.8, so they were exactly of courtship age, and only 30 percent of them were married. One particularly touching ad in the *Sunday Mercury* in 1862 carried a plea addressed to "patriotic unmarried ladies" from "a soldier, just returned from the wars. Have lost a leg, but expect to get a cork one; have a useless arm, but will be called brave for it; was once good-looking, but am now scarred all over." Some opportunists advertised in pairs: in Virginia's *Staunton Spectator* in March 1863, two "young gentlemen, who are both good-looking, intelligent, refined and tried soldiers of Jackson's army" announced their search for "any young ladies who may have a view of matrimony after the adjustment of existing difficulties"—a phrase which surely won an award for the greatest understatement of 1863.

New York Herald, *January 25, 1862*

Soldiers tended to be more willing to share personal details than other advertisers of the period—perhaps because, facing death, they saw no reason for evasion. In North Carolina's *Fayetteville Observer*, "Benny," who was a member of the 36th North Carolina Light Infantry and stationed in Fort Fisher, set out his straightforward wish list: "I am by no means very choice, it is a good wife I am after." Meanwhile, "Charles Wright, Louis Anderson, and Charles E., Headquarters, Excelsior Brigade, Second brigade, Second division, Third corps, Army of the Potomac" were together looking to make a match. All aged twenty, they had already served for three years; bear in mind, too, that the Excelsior Brigade fought some of the very deadliest battles of the Civil War, including Gettysburg. Imagine what these three friends had been through. No wonder they were looking for a happy distraction.

Those in the U.S. Navy found themselves in a similar predicament. Twenty-three-year-old William G. Baily placed an ad in August 1864 from the steamer the *Kanawha*, which was part of a blockade off Galveston, Texas. He described himself as "six feet in my stocking feet, black hair, hazel eyes, generally called good looking," who was after a woman "between the ages of 18 and 21, virtuous and a good housekeeper." Others at sea faced a number of logistical problems when it came to soliciting mail: for example, "Two young men of unexceptionable character, passably good looking, aged respectively twenty-two and twenty-five, who are fighting the battles of their country, having no lady friends whatever, wish to open a correspondence with two young ladies between the ages of eighteen and twenty-three, with a view to matrimony; good looks not absolutely necessary; must have a kind and pleasing dispositions." The problem was the address they offered to potential correspondents: "United States steamer *J.P. Jackson*, Western Gulf Blockading Squadron, Ship Island, or elsewhere." Note the crucial addition of "elsewhere." The reality was that they did not know where their ship would be in the coming weeks, such was the uncertainty of wartime conditions. Luckily, the U.S. Postal Service was highly efficient; President Abraham Lincoln considered it to be of such importance to the success of the war, in more ways than one, that he asked the U.S. postmaster general to appoint a special agent to oversee operations for the army and the navy.

The mystery is how any ensuing correspondence then played out. In one rare case, we know. In the early 2000s, Nancy L. Rhoades, the granddaughter of Edwin L. Lybarger, who had advertised from his hospital bed in

Kentucky, came across his officer's dispatch box hidden in an attic. Inside were scores of carefully folded, neatly organized letters. Some had the stamps torn off; some had been canceled by hand. They were all from women, nearly a quarter from women replying to the personal ad he placed, in which he sought female correspondents to help relieve "the monotony of camp life."

These letters are a treasure trove. It is incredibly rare to find a collection of letters from rural, middle-class women, who seldom left behind records of themselves. They offer an extraordinary insight into the experience of individual Northern women during the Civil War, as well as into the way they chose to construct their identity on paper.

Quickest on the uptake was twenty-one-year-old Jennie Hall of Logan, Ohio.

A picture of Jennie emerges gradually from her correspondence with Edwin, which lasted from July 1863 to March 1864 (there may have been more letters, possibly many more, but Edwin did not keep them). She was born in Urbana, Ohio, the youngest of ten children. Her father was a merchant but died when she was very young. She moved to New York City with her brother for a few years, where she attended school and "at times mingled in the gay whirls of fashionable society." But before long, her mother fell ill and she was summoned home to care for her. Possibly one of the reasons for her prolific letter-writing was the need to combat the desperate boredom brought on by becoming a full-time caregiver just when she felt she was at the height of her charms.

Jennie described herself as "5ft 4 inches—slender form neat and graceful. Black hair which curls beautifully. Black eyes noted for mischievousness. Round face—brunette complection. I am no beauty but passably good looking. Kind, generous, warmhearted, confiding, social, lively and very talkative." Her letters reveal she was fond of music, particularly singing and playing the piano; she occasionally asks Edwin to suggest a piece for her to learn. Her favorite poets were Thomas Moore and Lord Byron and she loved skating, too, when the weather was cold enough. It is a tantalizing glimpse of life on the Ohio home front.

In one letter, Jennie explained why she answered Edwin's ad in the first place:

I thought there would be something novel and interesting in corresponding with a gentleman whom I have never met. Another reason—and the main one—was to cheer the soldier who has gone forth bravely to fight the battles of this our "beloved country."

It probably also acted as a form of therapy to write to a stranger—to admit, as Jennie did, that "Oh the curses of this terrible war . . . How many hearts and homes made desolate." She did have concerns that "A gentleman might not in reality form a very exalted opinion of a young lady who would reply to an advertisement," but hopes "that no such thoughts have entered your mind during our correspondence which seems to be growing more and more interesting."

Edwin also hung on to many of the letters he received from twenty-two-year-old Lou Pearl Riggen, who lived in the countryside about five miles outside Mount Sterling, Kentucky.

Lou described herself as "a very plain girl, having gray eyes, brown hair, no freckles, and make no pretensions to beauty." She was from a Methodist family; her father died when she was young, followed not long afterward by her mother. Perhaps it is no coincidence that, like Jennie, she was free from parental control.

Lou liked to draw, but her true passion was reading. She enjoyed the historical works of Macaulay. She did not rate Dickens very highly, but was a fan of Victor Hugo. Poetry was where her heart lay though, in particular George Prentice's "The Closing Year" and Edgar Allan Poe's "The Raven." Favorite of all was Henry Wadsworth Longfellow's "The Song of Hiawatha": "The words flow so musically and the thoughts are in such charming unison with them," she wrote.

Like Jennie, Lou explained that she answered Edwin's ad because she "wanted novelty—or in other words—fun." Later in their correspondence, she clarifies that she hopes her letters "have fulfilled their object, that of rendering a little less monotonous the time of a federal soldier and of bringing interesting replies." She then emphasizes his "sublime heroism." The letters are deeply patriotic on both sides, expressing a love of country that no doubt fueled the desire to continue to nurture the relationship.

Edwin's correspondence with Lou lasted from September 1863 to February 1867. She was a more complex writer than Jennie: her letters are replete with heartfelt underlining, poetic descriptions of the weather, and moments of bickering over a small misunderstanding. Her tone also became increasingly flirtatious as she grew in confidence. For instance, after Edwin sent her a photograph of himself, she confided, "I thought you were very handsome indeed."

Like any respectable young woman, Lou found it proper to acknowledge possible concerns about her behavior: "Some of the staid newspaper writers are animadverting quite freely against the 'silly practice' of answering advertisements for correspondence." She then clarifies her intentions: "I like you as a correspondent, and I wrote to you because you were a soldier . . . I have no intention of embarking on the sea of marriage." She does admit though that she is enormously looking forward to meeting in person as soon as the war is over.

The relationship was soon so friendly that Edwin wrote to ask what she thought about a new idea of his. "Your idea of advertising for a wife is a happy one," she replied. "I have no doubt that every marriageable 'school marm' in Beaufort will respond with alacrity."

Lou's enthusiasm was perhaps not entirely genuine. The correspondence came to an abrupt end a few months later when he informed her that he was getting married, to which she replied in a panic, begging him to return all her letters as well as a photograph she had given him. He did not.

Civil War soldiers not only placed ads in significant numbers, but also replied to them, thereby casting personal ads in a new role as a form of public service: they provided the bored and the lonely with an epistolary outlet.

In 1862, Mary Ward Beecher, the niece of the *Uncle Tom's Cabin* author Harriet Beecher Stowe and the granddaughter of the Presbyterian minister Lyman Beecher, wrote to the *New York Herald* in search of a husband.

> Two young ladies, (a blonde and a brunette), educated in Paris, having property in Cuba, wish to make the acquaintance of two gentleman *sans reproche*. Address for one week Marie and Eugene Du Pont, Brookfield, Mass.

This was all a complete fantasy, of course; Mary blamed a friend for the idea, along with an "evil desire" to see her name in print. Reinventing herself as a Parisienne heiress was surely also part of the appeal.

She received over two hundred replies. The one that appealed to her the most came from a Wisconsinite named Major Louis Crane, who was in a hospital in Virginia recovering from a battle wound. "Take pity on me," he begged, "and lighten my dull home down here in Dixie."

The resulting six-month correspondence between Mary and Louis totaled over two hundred and fifty pages. Mary's letters were a source of comfort to Louis as he lay invalided; for her, they proved an enriching creative outlet, helping her define her own identity while also doing her patriotic duty to help a lonely soul.

His correspondence was defined by deception from the beginning. Mary was the first to embark on a false narrative, of course, with her talk of houses in Cuba, but her behavior was soon mirrored by Louis's. He made up the existence of a sister, then in a later letter got her name wrong. He defended himself thus:

> I endeavored to romance, in that letter, to my heart's content, and I haven't the slightest idea how many whoppers I told in it. I "went in" on the Cuban property style and I have now only a vague idea of flattering myself that I had succeeded. How little I dreamed of the pleasure this racy correspondence would give me, nor to what length it would grow.

Before long he lied again, writing of his sadness at his mother being dead, having only a few weeks earlier mentioned that she had sent him jellies.

The last straw, however, was when Louis joked that he had "learned that woman was deceitful above all things and desperately wicked." This led Mary to convey that she "now believe[d] you were married long ago." At that point she cut off the correspondence: she was only nineteen, and even in friendship it was not respectable to be exchanging news with an older married man, especially in view of her pedigree.

She was right. He was married. His justification was that "When I saw your advertisement . . . I supposed, and pardon me for saying too, that I had a right to suppose, that some romantic boarding-school damsel had been trying to procure a romantic correspondent and . . . some imp induced me answer it." To be fair, he had never claimed he was single and there was no hint of romance in the letters either of them wrote.

The upheaval and chaos created by the Civil War did, however, offer a number of opportunities to less scrupulous participants in the world of personal ads. In 1862, this ad appeared in a newspaper in Albany, New York:

> Wanted—a wife. A gentleman intending to start for Europe on Monday next, wishes to take w him a wife. Any young lady of pleasing address and appearance willing to perform the duties of a tender wife, will please address before noon tomorrow, R.J. Hall, Post Office.

Over sixty women replied, including one Annie Newton, who sent a daguerreotype and said she lived on Franklin Street near Ferry. The couple were married within a week.

The newlyweds headed to New York the same day; Mr. Hall was a clergyman, he said, and had pastoral calls to make. On that Sunday, he preached a sermon to a church in upper Manhattan, at which he implored the congregation to "give liberally to a man who had suffered for the cause of the Union." In an effort to solicit money, he claimed he was a recent refugee from his home state of Mississippi where he had fled when "His known attachment to the Union had excited the attention of his secession neighbors, who called on him and demanded money for the support of the rebel cause. He had none to give them and so they murdered his only child before his eyes, one of the rebels knocking out the child's brains with the butt of his musket."

This tragic tale turned out to be entirely untrue, however, and just an attempt to garner sympathy and raise some cash.

On April 9, 1865, General Robert E. Lee surrendered to Ulysses S. Grant on behalf of the Army of Northern Virginia, signaling the end of the Civil War. This was followed by a miserable reckoning of the devastation. Approximately 620,000 men had been killed—a generation decimated.

The war had a huge impact on the marital prospects of women everywhere. Between 1860 and 1890, unmarried women constituted a higher percentage of the population than at any other time in the nation's history. Finding a husband had become a trickier proposition than ever before. Most of the single young men who survived the war were not conventional marriage material: many had lost a limb, others were addicted to alcohol or drugs, while still more had contracted a venereal disease like syphilis or gonorrhea. Of those who did get through it relatively unscathed, thousands immediately headed west to start a new life on the frontier. Many women, therefore, had little option but to join them.

Fred

South Dakota, 1873

It was the pigs.

Esme had been over the night before. I used to pay her, but not anymore. Now I just asked her to carry on shaving her armpits to ensure the lice found a new home.

But in the morning she left, and it was just me and the pigs.

Feeding, cleaning out the sty, dealing with their illnesses, and, yes, talking to them. Out here on the plains. It could break a man's spirit.

All the while fearing the tribesmen would attack any moment. Pigs were worth something, especially mine, which would have won prizes in any fancy East Coast town. Shiny coats, noses that snuffled like the trains on the railroad shunting into town, eyes so bright they looked like stars in the sky.

So, yes, it was the pigs. I needed the help. It was tough living alone.

What I needed wasn't a couple of strong lads fresh off the railroad, like the pastor suggested.

It was a wife.

I quite liked the idea of some girl who chewed tobacco or wore bloomers, despite what the guys down the saloon said about the almost-certainly imaginary women they knew, despite what the newspapers said. Modern, they called them, with disgust, even fear. I, on the other hand, thought they sounded like a real companion. A friend, even. Fun, and jolly, and surprising.

A bit like my pigs.

And so, I decided to place an advertisement.

CHAPTER SIX

"ALL THEY REQUIRE IS TEETH": THE FRONTIER, C. 1850–1880

On a swelteringly hot June afternoon in 1871, a twenty-two-year-old seamstress named Sara Baines stepped down from a wagon in Fort Bridger, Wyoming. She was tired, dusty, and extremely nervous. She had traveled from Louisiana to make the acquaintance of a forty-six-year-old farmer named Jay Hemsley from Ohio. Of all the men who replied to the marriage ad she had placed in the October 12, 1869, edition of *Frank Leslie's Illustrated Newspaper*, she liked the sound of him the best. After writing to each other for more than a year, they agreed to meet.

And the day they met, they agreed to marry.

The ceremony was arranged for the following afternoon, June 5. It took place on the banks of the Green River, with the orange hawkweed in full bloom, and was conducted by the fort's minister; the bride wore a gray taffeta dress with black silk bows and carried a bouquet of wildflowers.

The couple then headed to Placerville, California, where they planned to open a general store.

Mr. and Mrs. Jay A. Hemsley

It is perhaps difficult to imagine a scenario in which traveling over a thousand miles across the country to the middle of nowhere to marry a man you had never met before seemed like the most appealing of all the options open to you. But for women like Sara Baines, that was the astonishing reality.

Between 1850 and 1880, population centers shifted west due to a continuing abundance of available and fertile land, decreased transportation costs, and increased population growth. Pioneers needed wives—and husbands—to establish families, populate the land, and fulfill the nation's Manifest Destiny. Marriage therefore acquired an additional practical importance outside the urban metropolises of the East Coast. Thousands of men trekked across the plains and the prairies in search of a new life but, once they settled and set up farms or businesses, they became in desperate need of help, ideally in the form of a woman who could be a wife, mother, and coworker combined. There was a general sense, as one observer put it in 1846, that "married persons are generally more comfortable, and succeed better, in a frontier country, than single men; for a wife and family, so far from being a burden to a western farmer, may always prove a source of pecuniary advantage in the domestic economy of his household." Marriage was, in many respects, an economic necessity. Particularly in the more isolated areas, however, suitable candidates were scarce. So marriage ads could at one time or another be found in almost every newspaper east of the Rocky Mountains.

Marriage ads reached Ohio by the 1840s, and within a decade they were in evidence across the border in Indiana too. In 1852, James Hanes turned to the *Richmond Palladium* to find "a lady worth a few thousand dollars, of common sense, with a taste for the fine arts, a lover of science, about the medium size, with an open, cheerful countenance, affectionate in disposition, and capable of taking care of a large family." In the *Indiana Herald* ten years later, "a young man of correct business habits" was looking for "any young lady of fair intellectual endowments, an ordinary share of beauty, who would not be averse to a personal superintendence of household matters." He almost—*almost*—manages to make the offer of becoming his unpaid housekeeper sound appealing.

These ads contain a far more extensive list of criteria than those of a hundred years earlier. It was no longer enough for a potential partner to be young, respectable, and solvent. The media's increasing emphasis on romantic love, underpinned by post-Enlightenment political and philosophical ideals that emphasized the importance of the pursuit of happiness, had made people choosier. The Western ethos emphasized the continued pursuit of happiness, as well as the importance of individualism, far more than other regions. Men did not want just any wife, but increasingly a wife who was well suited to them in terms of temperament and interests, as well as having the skills needed to survive the demands of the frontier.

For single women, particularly those in the East, marriage ads represented a thrilling opportunity. An article in Philadelphia's *Public Ledger* in 1837 detailed how,

> . . . the last census in Massachusetts shows a surplus of about 14,000 women, while that of the western states shows as great a preponderance of men. The young men of the northern and middle states swarm to the west, and leave the young women at home. The consequence is an unnatural state of society in both sections, the western men wanting wives and the eastern women wanting husbands . . . Every respectable young woman who goes west is almost sure of an advantageous marriage, while, from the superabundance of her own sex in the east, her chances for it are not greater than those for a disappointment.

This was the crux of the matter: "the superabundance of her own sex in the east." The plentitude of bachelors on the plains—and hence the chance for greater social and economic freedom away from home—beckoned women, many of whom had few other options.

No wonder some of these ads attracted a large number of replies. In 1854, a man advertising for a wife in Indiana received 794 letters in response, in addition to seventeen locks of hair, thirteen daguerreotypes, two gold rings, a thimble, and a copy of Ik Marvel's *Reveries of a Bachelor,* a bestselling 1850 book of nonfiction about life in rural America that Emily Dickinson counted among her favorites. According to the local newspaper, the advertiser "says that he is thoroughly convinced of the advantages of advertising."

In the same decade, ads became popular in Illinois, whose rural areas averaged one woman for every twenty-five men. Courtship rituals there were sometimes hasty, but at other times followed the more stylized rituals of the settled areas of the United States, where the man demonstrated his interest by paying a formal call on the woman and her family at her home. Church services, sporting events, lectures and clubs, dances and parties also provided matchmaking opportunities. But what happened when these mechanisms failed? In 1858 the *Olney Times* in Illinois carried an ad from "a middle-aged man, of industrious habits, kind disposition, and affectionate to children." He continued, "A proposition from a widow, with not more than one child, would be considered." Olney had a population of less than 1,500 people, so female company was limited.

North across the Illinois border, Wisconsin embraced marriage ads more enthusiastically than almost any other state. As early as 1839, just three years after the first white settlers arrived, three bachelor friends in Sheboygan, aged twenty-two, twenty-four, and twenty-seven, put a shout-out "to the single ladies of Wisconsin," the reason being that "there is a scarcity of single ladies hereabout." They were primarily looking for "those who understand all kinds of domestic housewifery," but they also had a complex set of physical requirements: "rather tall than short—rather slim than thick set—of good form and features—neat turned ankle and small feet, and not to exceed 18 years of age." It was also important they were "troubled with a little of the ready," an Irish phrase meaning possessing a bit of cash.

The three friends were probably Irish immigrants. Settlers were drawn to Wisconsin first by the fur trade, then by lead mining and, later, lumber. In the early years some intermarried with Native American women, but the increasing dominance of racist principles made white women preferable.

The problem was that almost all of the women in Wisconsin were either married or underage. A federal census taken the year after the ad was placed revealed almost twice as many men as women in a state with a population of just 30,000. David F. Sayre, a Wisconsinite who settled that same year, later asked, "The young girls, where were they? I have been trying to count them. I can remember but nine . . . [within] fifteen miles" of his house in Porter.

What was the solution? Some men made the trek East to find a wife in their native state. Others, like our three young Irish bachelors, turned to the newspapers for help. The Erie Canal was crucial to either approach, allowing news to travel quickly and easily from the Great Lakes to the East Coast, and women and men to travel back from it.

Advertising for a husband or wife grew with Wisconsin's population, as settlers flooded into the state. In Waukesha in 1855, a young man—"5 feet 11 inches in height, symmetrical in form, a dark hazel eye, and also a good and easy disposition"—sought a woman "not over 25 years of age, and understands all kinds of housework; she must have a good common education, as outward beauty would be of no consideration whatever. She must be neat and tidy about her dress, and also a believer in the Christian Religion. If she has $200 to put with what little he has got, it will tend to make things more comfortable." He added a crucial coda to his ad: "None but a true American woman would be accepted, for he is a true blue Yankee himself . . ." Almost all early settlers in Waukesha were descended from the Puritans who arrived in New England in the 1600s, so this seems to be an effort to maintain its racial uniformity.

The women of Wisconsin also chose to advertise, not owing to a lack of men, but rather a lack of suitable men. In other words, they asserted their right to be picky. Take this "Husband Wanted" ad:

Waukesha County Democrat, *August 8, 1855*

Seven years after the women's rights convention in Seneca Falls, this woman felt empowered enough to be highly prescriptive about her ideal husband: "I want no brainless dandy or foppish fool, but a practical man who can drive a coach or rock the cradle, hoe the garden or attend the ball-room." Don't we all, sweetheart.

By the late 1870s, the *Daily Milwaukee News*, the state's largest newspaper, carried personal ads nearly every day. This was despite the fact that the city of Milwaukee was famous for its many matchmaking opportunities such as concerts and dances, a direct result of the many highly musical German immigrants who fled the Revolution of 1848. The *Daily Milwaukee News* also featured ads from out of state, for example this one from a farmer in rural Michigan who took the creative step of advertising across the shores of a Great Lake for a companion:

Daily Milwaukee News, *April 21, 1878*

Directly to the west, a journalist for the *Dubuque Iowa News* declared in 1838 that, "So anxious are our settlers for wives that they never ask a single lady her age. All they require is *teeth*." The first settlers had arrived in Iowa just five years prior and men outnumbered women three to one, which was about average in these newly settled states.

Many newspapers in Iowa and elsewhere regularly encouraged women's immigration. In the *Davenport Courier* in 1855, one local correspondent remarked that "it would be an act of humanity if scores of the young maidens who are pining away in the eastern villages for somebody to love would set their faces at once toward Iowa." A few took the hint. In 1860, an ad appeared in the *Waterloo Courier* from a "young lady residing in one of the small towns in Central New York [who] is desirous of opening a correspondence with some young man in the West, with a view to matrimonial engagement . . . She is about 24 years of age, has a good disposition, enjoys good health, is tolerably well-educated, and thoroughly versed in the mysteries of housekeeping." Note how little she writes of her own desires—just a vague description of "some young man in the West"—but instead fills up her word count with a rundown of her own most appealing qualities. It is all about selling herself. The editor of the *Waterloo Courier* remarked that this notice presented "a rare chance for a young man to obtain that useful and essential article of household furniture—a wife."

Ads from women were sometimes subject to censure, unsurprisingly. Take one that appeared in the *St. Cloud Democrat* in Minnesota in 1860 from "a widow of 33 with a daughter of 17, and too far reduced in circumstances to enjoy the luxury of single blessedness longer in comfort . . . I have no relatives, I and my daughter are alone in the world. I should be glad to find a congenial companion and a home. I have been alone two years." A few days later, an opinion piece in the same newspaper delivered the following harsh judgment:

> We would be glad to think the writer is jesting; but if she is in earnest, have only to say that we would prefer standing sponsor for Mr. Buchanan's last veto and Mrs. Belzebub's next baby, to aiding such an arrangement. A woman who would thus huckster herself off, we would not touch unless with a long pole which we knew to be a good non-conductor. . . We . . . have more or less respect for every single

man in town, and would rather help to array him in a shroud than assist him into such a connection. Love-making is the men's business, and let them attend to it.

The reference to the devil's baby, as well as to President James Buchanan, who just a couple of weeks earlier had vetoed the Homestead Act, arguing that it went beyond the power of the federal government, reveals the author of the opinion piece to be a Republican of a conservative, religious bent.

But few took notice of such criticism. The matter of marriage was simply too important to leave to conservatives. The lack of established cultural norms in the West also meant that most of the time you could pretty much do what you wanted.

By the 1870s, ads were spreading even farther south and west. A Missouri farmer in 1875 advertised that he would reward anyone willing to marry him with three mules. In 1871, a Nebraska man was delighted by a photo he received from one correspondent, but when he traveled to Omaha to meet her, "Imagine his surprise in finding her very plain in features, in fact positively homely." (He married her anyway.) In Kansas, where the population increased by 6,500 people a year between 1865 and 1870, ads were especially popular:

> **Advertisement.**
> I wish to make the acquaintance of a lady of good character, between the ages of 22 and 30; good looking, good *disposition*, understands and likes housekeeping. Would like to live on a farm, and if understands music, please mention it. Object, matrimony if suited. Address,
>   A. B. COLLINS, Leavenworth, Kas.

Leavenworth Times, *October 13, 1870*

> Some gentleman of good family with some money and no vices can learn the address of a beautiful and accomplished petite brunette, anxious to have a beau. Object, matrimony. Address, for ten days, S. E. L. L., care REGISTER office.

Iola Register, *September 19, 1879*

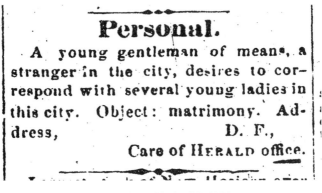

Kansas Herald, *April 2, 1880*

In 1879, a story in the *Weekly Kansas Chief* claimed that the circumstances it described proved that "it pays to advertise for a wife." But the narrative was not quite as straightforward as the paper said.

William Mayhew of Centralia, Nemaha County, Kansas, "a substantial, respectable farmer, in good circumstances, engaged extensively in stock-raising," decided one day to advertise for a wife. He received a large number of replies: "Some were from young girls, who wrote to have a little fun; others were from women who were in earnest; while still others were from condemned stock, who wished to palm themselves off on an honest man. But Mr. Mayhew was no fool . . ." While visiting one of them, he happened to hear of a woman who had not answered his ad but who sounded perfect for him. Her name was Nancy E. Bell and she was a widow and "a business woman, who has long resided on a stock farm, and has managed it herself for the past five or six years." In the newspaper's opinion, "She is perhaps the most suitable woman that Mr. Mayhew could have found." They were married on July 27, 1879.

Happy tales of this sort were frequently reprinted in local newspapers all over the nation, raising awareness of personal ads and contributing to their popularity.

Between 1865 and 1870, the number of newspapers in Kansas increased from thirty-seven to eighty, as was typical of developments nationwide. In 1800, there were two hundred newspapers in the United States; by 1860 this figure had risen to three thousand. Soon almost every town had its own paper, in large part due to the rise of the penny press which hugely expanded the circulation opportunities. Combined with the increase in public education under President Andrew Jackson between 1829 and 1837, which produced a more literate republic, the spread of information was increasingly democratized.

The rapid expansion of ads to the West was made possible by the concurrent development of the nation's infrastructure—in particular, of the railroads.

The railroads played a crucial role in the mail service. They were first used to distribute the mail in Pennsylvania in 1832; within six years, all railroads were designated post routes. From then on, the postal system expanded hugely, increasing not only the number of people who could answer ads but also the circulation of the newspapers in which the ads appeared. Beyond the East Coast, communication remained a problem up until 1860 with the launch of the Pony Express, with hardy young riders carrying letters from Missouri to California. It lasted only nineteen months before it was supplanted by the telegraph.

The joining of the tracks of the First Transcontinental Railroad at Promontory, Utah, on May 10, 1869, ushered in a new era of exchange between east and west of not only mail and goods but also people. Thousands of men and women, especially immigrant single women, chugged west toward the prairies and the plains. The railroads had a particularly strong impact on the Dakotas. In 1872, the Dakota Southern Railroad completed its main line between Vermillion and Sioux City, Iowa, a distance of 37 miles, while that same year the Northern Pacific Railway reached Fargo. Marriage ads from this period offer a vivid sense of the challenges faced by settlers there. In 1882, a woman in Mandan, North Dakota, wrote to the local paper just a couple of days after she buried her dead husband: "It is coming on spring now, and I am a lone woman with a big ranch and the Indians about. I don't mind the Indians, the red devils, but I have too much work for any woman to do . . ." She wanted "a steady man [who] likes work, and wants a good home."

Laura Ingalls Wilder, author of *Little House on the Prairie*, heard from her father, a local justice, about a woman who had turned up in the town of Walnut Grove in Minnesota, demanding to be married immediately to a man whose personal ad she had answered. Some years later, Laura's daughter, Rose Wilder Lane, turned it into a piece in the *Saturday Evening Post* called "Object Matrimony" (1934).

"Object Matrimony" opens with a description of the railroad in a border town "at the end of the line" in Sioux County, North Dakota: "Steel-rails had reached the town-site two weeks earlier. Now a train came every day." Sure enough, that afternoon was no different.

> The iron horse came snorting, clanging, and with a clashing jerk it halted. . . . Men shouted greetings to engineer, brakeman, fireman, they hailed acquaintances looking out of immigrant cars; the bell clanged, the whistle tooted, boys yelled. But silence spread around the girl who stepped down from the passenger coach . . . She was graceful, slender, and hardly yet an old maid . . .

Her name is Clarinda; she is nineteen and from South Duxbury, Massachusetts. She heads first to the county clerk to obtain a marriage license, then to the home of her intended paramour, a twenty-two-year-old local boy named Jedediah Masters.

On their first night together, Clarinda tells Jedediah, "It's a fair bargain. You advertised for a wife because you wanted a woman, any woman. I married you because I wanted a husband." Theirs ends up being a pretty happy partnership, but twenty years later, the truth emerges: it turns out Clarinda fell into Jedediah's arms just to avoid being jilted by her fiancé back home in Massachusetts before he could elope with her sister.

Border towns like those in Sioux County existed almost solely to secure U.S. control over Native American lands. It was therefore in the interests of the federal government to encourage marriage, and the population growth that would follow, through its land policies. In 1877, the Desert Land Act was passed to promote the settlement of arid lands through immigration in the Dakotas, as well as all the western states: a married couple could get up to 640 acres of land for free (320 acres for a single individual), as long as they provided proof of irrigation within three years and improvements worth $1.25 per acre. This policy could only succeed in the long term, however, if there were enough women to help work the land, as well as—crucially—to procreate.

Real-life equivalents of Clarinda came to be known as mail-order brides, a reductive term that implies that the women involved were entirely passive victims in the enterprise. Often the gamble they took worked out well, as in the case of Sara Baines, whom we met at the beginning of this chapter. She and her new husband Jay settled in Placerville, California, a "gold rush" town named after the placer gold deposits found in the area's hills and rivers in the late 1840s. They ran a popular general store named Hemsley Mercantile and were happily married for no less than fifty-one years. Sometimes, however, the gamble did not work out quite so well, as we shall see.

Emma

New York City, 1872

The problems all started when I ran out of money.

I could speak French and German, play the piano and sing, beat anyone at draughts, and pick a hat to suit even the plainest of women. But I had absolutely no idea how to pay for a roof over my head.

It hadn't mattered while my father was alive. But then he tripped over a stray turkey whilst crossing the road one rainy day and ended up under the wheels of the Governor's coach.

After that, everything changed.

What I needed was a man to marry me. A respectable man—kind, with some cash.

The difficulty was that on the rare occasions I did meet men, I had little way of ascertaining what they were worth. In dollars, that is. Sure, I could check out their clothes and their carriage, but many a charlatan had conned their way into a woman's heart that way. And I couldn't afford to waste my time.

So it occurred to me to lay all my cards on the table (I had always had excellent luck at cards). I read the ads in the New York Times *every day, and so did all my friends. Maybe that was my way out of this mess? I had always been the conventional type, but this was different. I was desperate.*

And so, I decided to place an advertisement.

CHAPTER SEVEN

"A Love of a Mustache": New York City, c. 1840–1880

You may sit in a New York Restaurant in the morning for a few hours, and you will observe that the very first thing each man does, before ordering his breakfast, is to call for the *Herald*—and the next thing he does is to look at the top of the first column and read the "Personals" . . . There is such a toothsome flavor of mystery about them! It is the whole secret.

—Mark Twain, 1867

M aybe Miss Sarah Redmond had Mark Twain's words in mind when she headed into the office of the *New York Herald* to place a personal ad.

Wanted: a husband; would like to marry a gentleman of comfortable circumstances residing in the south. S.E.R., Herald up-town office.

Sarah had been born in Brooklyn, a middle child in between her older sister Mary and her younger brother James; her mother was a native New Yorker, but her father was an Irish immigrant who died when she was a toddler, and a stepfather, Thomas, quickly arrived on the scene. In 1879, when Sarah's ad appeared in the *Herald*, Mary had recently left home to get married; was her stepfather impatient for Sarah to hurry up and do the same to free him from the burden of supporting her?

Sarah received several replies to her ad, among them one postmarked Hawkinsville, Georgia, from a farmer who described himself as middle-aged and well-off. After corresponding for a couple of months, Sarah agreed to marry him.

Accompanied by her mother and James, Sarah traveled by train to Georgia and then transferred to a stagecoach. After riding for hours over a rough, unpaved road, it was nearly midnight when they pulled up in front of a ramshackle log cabin in the middle of nowhere. Her brother knocked forcefully on the door while the two women hovered nervously behind him.

They heard someone inside shuffling slowly along the passageway. An elderly, gray-haired, frail-looking man opened the door. One look at him confirmed that he was clearly neither middle-aged nor well-off.

Sarah Redmond had been conned.

"The mother became wrathy, and the brother let fly a few not very complimentary remarks . . . The surprise of the young lady when she saw that her lover was an old wreck of humanity rather than a young and handsome southerner can only be imagined," recounted a reporter for the *Atlanta Constitution*, who happened upon the trio at the station a few hours later as they waited—exhausted, embarrassed, and angry—for a train to take them back to New York to continue the hunt for a husband.

❧

New York City experienced a period of astonishingly rapid growth during the mid-19th century. In the 1850s, the ship tonnage passing through the port increased by 60 percent. The number of trolleys rose from 255 in 1846 to 683 in 1853, by which date they were carrying over 100,000 passengers a day. By 1852, 2.5 million passengers a year were arriving in the city by the Harlem, Hudson, and New Haven railroad lines. Gold flowed in, too: $175 million worth between 1851 and 1854 alone. Banks popped up everywhere: there were twelve in 1851, and sixty by 1855, many of them housed in grand purpose-built structures made of New Jersey brownstone and cast-iron columns. All told, one in fifteen of all those employed in U.S. manufacturing worked on the island of Manhattan.

The intersection of Broadway and Canal Street typified the city's hustle and bustle: "Faces and coats of all patterns, bright eyes, whiskers, spectacles, hats, bonnets, caps, all hurrying along in the most apparently inextricable confusion. One would think it a grand gala day. And it's rather overpowering to think of that rush and whirl being their regular every-day life," wrote the social reformer Charles Loring Brace.

"Broadway" by W. S. L. Jewett, from Harper's Weekly, *February 15, 1868*

This was a city starkly divided between rich and poor, with everyone acutely aware of their place in the social order.

Marriage ads reached their apogee in mid-19th century New York. Prominent champions of the genre included the *New York Herald* and, later, the *New York Times*, which came to dedicate an entire column to these "particolored, broken and incoherent phrases of human passion," as one journalist described them. Not only was this section of the newspaper wildly entertaining, it also offered New Yorkers a much-needed matchmaking service. Ads themselves evolved, too, demonstrating an increasingly complex and creative lexicon and beginning to reflect specifically Victorian attitudes toward love and marriage.

The continuing increase in the number of personal ads editors chose to include in their papers was in part a result of the fierce rivalry between New York's penny presses. The *New York Sun* printed its first edition in 1833, followed in 1835 by the *New York Herald* and in 1841 by the *New York Tribune*. To be profitable, a penny press needed to attract readers from all sections of society. Aiming the content at both sexes, unlike the more male-oriented commercial press, was one way to do this; another was the inclusion of titillating personal ads. Take this one, which appeared in the *Sun* in 1840:

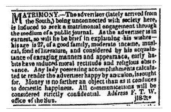

The advertiser is in his mid-twenties, new in town, lacking contacts, and has sensibly decided to go public in his search for a wife. In short, he possesses many of the same attributes as other advertisers of the period not only in Philadelphia and Boston, but also across the Atlantic in London and Liverpool.

By the mid-1840s, marriage ads were a semi-regular feature of Horace Greeley's *New York Tribune*, too. An ad from 1845 described "a gentleman about 30 years of age, possessing a moderate fortune, [who] is desirous of connecting himself in matrimony with some respectable lady who is willing to undertake the charge of a small household." In other words, he is after an unpaid housekeeper.

But it was the *New York Herald* (later the *New York Herald Tribune*) that deserved the most credit for popularizing the modern personal ad.

The *Herald's* founder, James Gordon Bennett Sr., believed the role of a newspaper was "not to instruct but to startle and amuse." Established in 1835, it made its name with sensationalist coverage of the murder of prostitute Helen Jewett. Bennett was also among the first to spot the entertainment value of ads, a significant turning point in the history of advertising.

His newspaper's earliest marriage ad, from "Maria," appeared on October 29, 1835, just days after American settlers in Texas, at the time governed by Mexico, fired their first shots asserting their independence.

A couple of weeks later, Bennett received a mysterious wedding invitation, which he eventually worked out was from the "Maria" in the ad and her speedily gained fiancé as a way of thanking him for helping facilitate their romance.

Within ten years of launching, the *New York Herald* was the most popular daily in America. By 1853, it boasted a readership of about 53,000, and by 1860 personal ads appeared in it every day. Most of the men who advertised were educated and middle-class—that is, the sort of men who described themselves as "a gentleman, aged 26, of fair personal appearance and unexceptionable position, who neither drinks, smokes nor chews." They advertised for many of the same reasons they did in New York in the 1780s, or Philadelphia in the 1840s, or on Tinder today, most commonly because they are "strangers in the city" or even "a stranger in [their] native city," so fast was the pace of change. They have traveled from every corner of the nation: from San Francisco, from Richmond, from New Orleans—the latter being "detained North on business, and no lady acquaintances"—as well as a "gentleman of 30, college graduate and practical mining engineer, who has spent the last ten years in the Western territories . . ."

The ads offer a vivid glimpse into the loneliness experienced by many New Yorkers. "A young gentleman" writes that he is "wearied of hotels and boarding houses," as does a "lonely widower" who is "weary of solitary rooms." An eighteen-year-old-girl agreed, saying she was "wearied of a life of single blessedness," while a "widowed lady" is "tired of living alone." As one young buck explained in his ad, "New York, though so large, is, as to sociability, a desert to a great many; and it often renders single life exceedingly heavy, and marriages difficult, for the frequent mutual unfitness of limited chance acquaintances." Many others shared the sentiment but expressed it in a different literary form. "For eight weary months, I have met in the crowded streets but two faces I have ever seen before," observed Lydia Maria Child, concluding that in the city, "the loneliness of the soul is deeper, and far more restless, than in the solitude of the mighty forest."

What did the male population of New York look for in a wife? A "young lady not over 24, possessing some wealth, refinement, intelligence and an amiable disposition" is a standard request. Others sought "a lively, goodhearted, romping, skating and loveable young lady" or a "kind-hearted wife, a friend, a companion for life." This newfound emphasis on being "loveable" or a "companion" is evidence of an increasing belief in the importance of romantic feeling in making a marriage work. Some, meanwhile, continued to be open about the transactional nature of marriage, for example the gentleman looking for "a lady with some capital to form a business and matrimonial partnership. Being interested in a lucrative old established business, he wants to buy it out. Rare chance to acquire happiness and fortune honestly."

The language of personal ads evolved considerably during this period. There was a new enthusiasm for quoting from a famous book or poem, perhaps as a way of asserting identity. One advertiser paraphrased Dante's *La Vita Nuova*: "Romance will never see its end, nor a noble heart half its treasure. So says the poet." Another referenced Shakespeare's *Richard III*, seeking a woman "who will make the winter of his discontent glorious summer." Ads were becoming wittier and more creative; as the genre became familiar to readers, it was easier to have some fun with it.

One Thursday morning in 1861, a woman named Ethel placed an ad for a husband in the *New York Herald*. She explained that she was "compelled to adopt this mode of opening a correspondence owing to the strict surveillance under which she is placed at home." The successful candidate needed to be under twenty-five and "possess a fine intellectual countenance, be of an agreeable disposition, and above all have a love of a mustache." Anyone interested was asked to write to her immediately, care of the Brooklyn post office.

Most of the women who advertised in the *New York Herald* were, like Ethel, openly seeking some kind of practical help, in particular financial support. There was the "widow lady of respectability and agreeable manners [who] desires to meet with a gentleman of good standing and means to support a wife," as well as the "stranger in the city, alone and friendless" looking for "a gentleman . . . to whom she could look for protection, with a view to matrimony at some future time" who was "willing to give her immediate assistance." Some are more specific in their demands. One young woman sought an "elderly" gentleman because she would "rather be 'an old man's darling than a young man's slave.'" A twenty-year-old confessed "she has been directed by her spirit friends to take this method of procuring a suitable companion for life." Another was looking not just for a sea captain, but for a sea captain who supported slavery:

> AN AMERICAN LADY, 19 YEARS OLD, IS LOOKING for a husband between the ages of thirty-five and fifty; must not object to children, as the advertiser has a male child to care for; would prefer a sea captain; no objection to a widower if possessed of a kind heart and means. No abolitionist need apply. Address, inclosing carte de visite if convenient, Fanny, box 201 Herald office.

Meanwhile, in 1857 "Miss Fannie De F. Le S." of Poughkeepsie, New York, "disgusted with fortune hunters and insincere friends," announced to readers of the *Herald* her desire to meet any "gentleman matrimonially inclined" who was willing to "give her a true, manly Heart in exchange for a fortune and a wife." As the American middle classes evolved, placing a personal ad was one way to assert one's position within the social strata.

In light of the paucity of options available to women like Fannie, it is no wonder that contemporary novels often depicted them suffering from a kind of sickness. The sickness was boredom; the response, rage. As Charlotte Chesebro, one of the most innovative women writers of the period, put it in *The Children of Light*, her 1853 novel about two women who find themselves disappointed by the limitations of love:

> I feel like rushing out . . . But here I am, only a woman—a house-keeper . . . to be kept in my "proper sphere" and "place," and never to stir an inch out of it in any direction, for fear that all creation would turn against me, and hunt me down, as they would a wild beast!

No wonder some chose to rebel, refusing to be passive onlookers in their own lives, preferring instead to strike out alone to find a partner and build a life for themselves.

By 1855, a census of New York City put the population at just under 630,000 and rising fast. As the nation's leading port and manufacturing center, migrants flocked there from all over the world in search of a new life. But there was a significant gender imbalance. Up until 1830, the ratio of women to men had been about even, but within a decade there averaged 125 women of marrying age for every 100 men. Although a lot of young men arrived in the city as transatlantic immigrants, the nature of the urban labor market meant that even more left again in search of employment on farms and elsewhere; for young women, employment opportunities were mostly local and the prospects outside New York limited.

Eliciting a marriage proposal could therefore be tricky. Contemporary conduct literature such as *Marriage and the Duties of the Marriage Relations* by G. W. Quinby (1852) and *The Lady's Guide to Perfect Gentility* by Emily Thornwell (1857) stipulated that the ideal age for a woman to marry was between twenty and twenty-five, so is it any wonder that even those only just out of their teens sometimes harbored a fear of spinsterhood?

On the plus side, the expansion of respectable wage work for New York women beyond domestic service into fields like retail and teaching offered many the opportunity to liberate themselves from their parents. This meant they could merrily flout some of the social conventions that had previously restricted their behavior, including the way they found a husband.

By 1861, the popularity of the *New York Herald*'s personals lay at the very heart of its continuing success, and the paper published a prominent editorial singing their praises:

> Who is there who does not read the "Personals" of the *Herald*, and who can read them without having his mind directed into channels of romance? . . . this column of the daily newspaper contains within itself a most curious phantasmagoria of city life, and those who have a taste for real romance need go no farther to gratify it.

The ads offered nosy New Yorkers a glimpse into their neighbors' private lives, and in this way were a little like a hundred-word version of best-selling sentimental novels of the period such as Maria Cummins's *The Lamplighter* (1854), the story of an orphan rescued from her abusive guardian by a lamplighter, which sold 20,000 copies in its first twenty days. Except that the ads were real.

From 1866 onward, as the number of subscribers to the *New York Herald* topped 80,000, personal ads started to be printed on its front page, where they remained until the 20th century. As it was the most widely read newspaper in the nation, the impact on the American cultural consciousness was significant.

Personal ads had become so popular in New York that they started to appear in even the most niche publications. Take the *Water-Cure Journal*, aimed at those keen on hydrotherapy and other forms of alternative medicine, which by mid-century claimed an astonishing circulation of 50,000. Part of its appeal were the personal ads from people in search of a vegetarian partner, and many felt distinctly modern for the period, for example the one from a woman who "wears the Bloomers when she can" and is looking for "a practical anti-slavery man, anti-tobacco, and I care not if anti-razor."

And what about the city's paper of record? Where was the *New York Times* in all of this?

In 2001, the *New York Times* announced in a press release that it had decided to feature personal ads "for the first time in its history." This was entirely untrue. From the 1850s through the 1890s, hundreds of ads appeared in its pages. Only a handful have seen the light of day since.

The first issue of the *New York Times* (initially known as the *New-York Daily Times*) appeared on September 18, 1851. It stated its intention thus: "We shall be *Conservative*, in all cases where we think Conservatism essential to the public good; and we shall be *Radical* in everything which may seem to us to require radical treatment and radical reform." Within ten days, the *Times* had acquired a readership of over 10,000, including everyone from "business men in their stores" to "the most respectable families in town," according to cofounder Henry Raymond.

Just over a year later, the paper published its first marriage ad:

New York Times, *November 29, 1852*

The ad, which appeared on November 29, 1852, a few days after Franklin Pierce was elected the fourteenth president of the United States, is from "a young gentleman, of respectable appearance and address, having formed a business connection sufficiently remunerative to warrant the extension of his social relations." Romantic, huh? He is looking for a wife of "modesty, morality, and strict neatness," and goes on to suggest that he has placed the ad primarily for the purposes of efficiency: "Any lady willing to forego the frivolities of a silly courtship for the more immediate prospect of a sensible marriage" is encouraged to get in touch. One wonders whether anyone responded to this exceedingly pragmatic invitation.

Thereafter, the *New York Times* featured about one personal ad a week, apart from 1860 to 1868, when a dedicated matrimonial column resulted in more. One early advertiser, "Bertram," laid out the case for them, condemning "the narrow bigotry and conventionalities of society, which, by interposing barriers to the free intercourse of the sexes, and thus limiting our choices, condemn multitudes of even the most favored to lives of celibacy and misery." He exhorts readers to "rise above the prejudice of mode and tyranny of custom in the search for happiness, and in the hope of escaping the relentless social constriction which crushes our best aspirations within the folds of its 'circles' and thus dooms us to become the helpless victims of mere matrimonial chance or accident." No doubt many shared his frustration with the restrictive social etiquette of the day.

The personal ads in the *New York Times* were placed by a different set than those in the *New York Herald*. They are of a grander sort, among them a "young gentleman who is about to graduate at New-England college," a twenty-four-year-old owner of a dry goods importer, and a "young, able politician, capable of going to the United States Senate" who expressed his need for "a matrimonial alliance with a young, wealthy lady; a political writer preferred."

In general, though, readers of the *New York Times* wanted the same sort of wife as everyone else: "young, pretty and intelligent." What is entirely new, however, is the emphasis on the home. Take Willie Sumpter, "lately from the South," "engaged in the mercantile business down town" and looking for "a young lady of good family, who is amiable, pretty and intelligent." He goes on:

> Believing that the great object of life is the attainment of domestic happiness, and that it cannot exist where there is not a congeniality of tastes and dispositions, the advertiser would state that his tastes and habits are such that his home would be to him the source of all his happiness.

Willie is echoed by many other advertisers, who similarly sought a woman "who would rather enjoy the comfort and blessings of a happy though humble home than the frivolities and fleeting pleasures of a fashionable life" (1860) or was "disposed to make a home comfortable and happy for her husband" (1861). This represents a typically mid-19th century emphasis on the sacred nature of private space, as opposed to public space.

Ads became so popular that one advertiser in the *Times* commented, "this method of procuring a wife is, to use an expression more forcible than elegant, entirely 'run into the ground.'" He goes on to express his concern that "he hopes that his predecessors in this line have not appropriated all the young, pretty and intelligent girls throughout the length and breadth of the land . . ."

And what about the women who placed ads in the pages of the *Times*?

"Without beauty to attract the world's crowd, or gold to allure the fortune hunter, I am, I believe, a true-hearted, refined, educated woman—young, frank, and mirthful, with the birthright entrée of cultured circles" ran an ad from a Miss Ward in the *New York Times* in 1859. It is perhaps surprising that she does not also include "honesty" in her list of attributes.

New York Times, *December 21, 1859*

There was also much chatter over an ad in 1861 from "a stylish young Parisienne, recently arrived, [who] has found herself suddenly thrown out of occupation, and seeks some honorable means of subsistence."

New York Times, *October 12, 1861*

She sought the acquaintance of "some sincere American gentleman, of middle age and permanent business, with a view to marriage. The advertiser is an excellent musician and linguist, is of pleasant disposition, and has much personal attraction; is a good house-worker, and can make a home cheerful."

The matter of marriage was increasingly incorporated into the city's pervasive culture of commerce. In 1846, America's first department store, A.T. Stewart & Co. (nicknamed the Marble Palace due to its white marble façade), opened its doors on the east side of Broadway between Chambers and Reade Streets. Within fifteen years, sales peaked at an average take of $20,000 a day. Among the proprietor's many innovations was to minimize the role of the shop assistant, who had in the past brought all the goods out from behind the counter for customers to see; shoppers were instead encouraged to stroll around at leisure, picking up and examining everything on offer themselves. It was in many ways not dissimilar to what women did when they perused the pages of the *New York Times* to find a husband. New York was experiencing a revolution in the way women shopped for clothes, so why not husbands?

With personal ads now a regular feature of New York's paper of record, it was all but inevitable that they would attract censure. In the same way that you hear people today saying of Tinder, "Whatever happened to meeting at a dinner party?" the more personal ads were seen to subvert middle-class norms of matchmaking, the more mainstream society—which is always wary of change, especially change that makes people feel out of touch or left behind—feared them. In 1860, *Vanity Fair* commented sardonically:

> After this, good people, buy your wives and husbands at the livery establishments, as you would horses, dogs, etc. No more courting, flirting, bother, disappointment and wounded feelings. Step up to the office, examine the stock, take your pick, pay your money and drive to the parson. Hurrah for progress!

Some of the strongest criticism of personal ads came from the country's highest-paid newspaper columnist, Fanny Fern, who was famous for having coined the phrase, "The way to a man's heart is through his stomach." Her column for the *New York Ledger* (a rival of the *Times* and the *Herald*) was widely syndicated across the country, and in 1857 she launched a lengthy attack on people who placed personal ads. It was not the men's involvement to which she objected: "That prurient young men, and broken-down old ones, should seek amusement in matrimonial advertisements, is not so much a matter of surprise." It was the women's: "There is no necessity for an attractive, or, to use a hateful phrase, a 'marketable' woman, to take such a degrading step . . . A woman must first have ignored the sweetest attributes of womanhood, have overstepped the last barrier of self-respect, who would parley with a stranger on such a topic . . ." With this, Fern betrays a profound misunderstanding of the challenges many women faced in trying to find a husband. On the other hand, she does also establish the template for a hardy perennial topic for newspaper columnists: the gleeful expression of disapproval of advertising for love.

One might think Fern would have some sympathy for women who took charge of their own marital destiny. After being left destitute following the death of her first husband, Fern immediately remarried—only to abandon her second husband amid great scandal a couple of years later when she fell in love with her publisher (with whom she then lived happily for the rest of her life).

Journalist James McCabe in his 1869 book about New York, *The Secrets of the Great City*, went even further than Fern in his condemnation. In his view, "By far the greatest number of advertisements of this kind are inserted by persons who wish to levy black mail upon those who are foolish enough to reply to them." Apocryphal or not—he offers up no evidence—he was putting forward a commonly held view.

McCabe was certainly correct that some of the ads were scams, probably more so in New York than anywhere else, partly due to the sheer volume that appeared in the papers every day, but also to the number of innocents, new in town and vulnerable to abuse. Between 1840 and 1860, more than three million immigrants passed through the city. Walt Whitman noted that "Every great city is a sort of countryman-trap. Accordingly there are here in New York various kinds of scamps who do business upon the inexperience of strangers; and accounts are continually appearing in the papers of this or that sojourner robbed, swindled, and perhaps beaten, in consequence of inexperience, usually, however, tinged a little with what looks very much like folly."

Scams surrounding personal ads took various forms. Some were indeed the kind of blackmail McCabe described. Others involved men misrepresenting their marital or financial status; Sarah Redmond, whom we met at the beginning of this chapter, was a victim of this. The problem with personal ads has always been that it is impossible to know if people really are who they say they are, even more so the more popular and widespread ads became.

In 1855, the mayor of New York, Fernando Wood, described by a contemporary as "the handsomest man I ever saw, and the most corrupt man that ever sat in the Mayor's chair," received a letter pleading for help. It told a pitiful story of a fourteen-year-old girl who had secretly answered an ad in the *New York Herald* from a man claiming to be a wealthy widower on the lookout for "a lady of education and refinement for a wife; not very particular about her age." According to the girl's mother, who wrote the letter, "All at once I saw her shape alter and her lively spirits gone . . ." Her daughter had not only fallen pregnant, but then discovered her lover was married with four children. "Do Sir, all in your power, to make the press not advertise such people's business," she implored.

The following year, the *Times* reported on the case of "a great scoundrel" from Philadelphia who "patronized the matrimonial department of the New York papers." He repeatedly advertised for a wife under the pseudonym Calvin Luther, resulting in him forming relationships with dozens of women, among them "J.A.B., West 15th Street; S.H.C., Union-square; C.C., Brunswick, N.J.; Fanny C., Northumberland; Grace C., New-Haven; Matilda S., Mattason; Alice F., Plattsburg, N.Y.; Clara H.; W.H.; L.M., Brooklyn; Rebecca M.; Mary M., Brooklyn; W.M., Williamsburg; M. La P., Williamsburg; Mrs. B.E.L., Union-square; Beatrice M., Hoboken; Grace O., New-York; Emily R., Sullivan-place; Josephine S., East Broadway; W.S." Behind each and every name lies a woman betrayed.

The *Times* had in its possession some of the letters these women wrote to Calvin Luther. The one from "Pauline" sounds as if she has been reading too many sentimental novels: "the master passion of my soul is an intense yearning for affection. I crave sympathy and kindness, and would deeply repay such by the devotion of a heart formed to feel and reciprocate every tender emotion, a heart capable of experiencing a love unbiased by all selfish considerations, whose chief gratification would arise from the welfare and happiness of the beloved object." Having presented herself as the very embodiment of the perfect Victorian wife, she immediately undermines herself by boldly suggesting he meet her "at the Hamilton Ferry (New-York) in the ladies room between 3½ and 4 o'clock in the afternoon" where she will be wearing "a red shawl, green shirred crepe bonnet, and black lace veil."

The rogue fled to Australia before the police could arrest him, but according to the *Times* he "has left behind sorrowing and forsaken a host of women, who, smitten by his charms, lost their hearts and—some of them—a considerable quantity of money, besides other things of more or less value" (an oblique reference to their virginity).

The *Times* concluded, optimistically, that "We trust the revelations of this case will check the somewhat active business that has been done for some months past in the line of advertising for wives." It did not.

By 1865, it was not uncommon for the *Times* to feature a couple of tales a day of fraud perpetrated through the personals. Take May 15, when the front page carried a gleeful report of the capture of Jefferson Davis, the president of the Confederacy, under the headline "Davis' Camp Surprised at Daylight . . . He Put On His Wife's Petticoats and Tries to Sneak into the Woods . . ." That same day, there was a story about a photographer named Crawford placing marriage ads in which he claimed to be a captain in the navy, luring women from as far south as Virginia and as far west as Chicago. Meanwhile, letters from a vulnerable young woman in Mittineague, Massachusetts, asking for the $20 fare to New York in exchange for becoming the advertiser's mistress turned out to be the work of a Miss Armstrong, who was supporting her entire family with this income stream. In the view of the *Times*, "This system should be broken up, and honest newspaper publishers should refuse favors of this character." Apparently, the editorial department of the newspaper had no idea what the advertising department was up to.

Between 1860 and 1900, the population of New York City more than doubled. The increasingly crowded and public nature of life in New York's urban, industrial environment meant that even the search for love was no longer a uniformly private affair. To some, this presented advantages. In *The Bostonians* by Henry James (1886), the personals are a symbol of success for publicity-seeking Selah Tarrant, as well as an attractive form of exposure: "The newspapers were his world, the richest expression, in his eyes, of human life; and, for him, if a diviner day was to come upon earth, it would be brought about by copious advertisement in the daily prints. He looked with longing for the moment when [his daughter] Verena should be advertised among the 'personals.'" A personal ad allowed you to stand out from the crowd for the day and experience the thrill of seeing your own words in print. You could control your own narrative, describing yourself however you saw fit.

Annie

Chicago, 1873

My little girl needed a father.

Not to pretend I did it just for her. I needed some fun. Any kind of fun. I saw my married friends heading out on the most extraordinary excursions: a debate on women's rights at the town hall, a concert by a visiting opera singer, a day out on a riverboat. It didn't feel fair.

Nobody in Chicago knew that, back home in my town, my doctor had got me pregnant. They all thought he had saved me from influenza and was to be worshipped and adored.

The truth was, he had sentenced me to a life in exile from my family. The scandal, you see.

To celebrate my twentieth birthday last week, I took my daughter to feed the ducks. We mostly ate stale bread anyway, so it worked out well.

But it was not the life I wanted.

One day, I tied the ribbon on my fraying green bonnet, took my daughter to the twelve-year-old next door who sometimes watched her for me, ran for the tram across the street, and off to downtown I went.

I thought about my predicament the entire bumpy ride there.

My little girl needed a father.

And so, I decided to place an advertisement.

CHAPTER EIGHT

"Object: Fun and Perhaps Matrimony": Chicago, c. 1865–1900

1883

Twenty-eight-year-old Augusta Larson shifted restlessly from foot to foot. She had been waiting for more than four hours in the immigration line at Castle Garden, the main processing center for new arrivals to New York.

All around her, babies screamed in their mothers' arms. Children tried to nap on the cold stone floor. The family in front shuffled off for a bath, which had recently been made a requirement for entry to prevent the spread of disease.

Augusta had been violently seasick on the eight-week passage from Sweden, and still felt so weak that it was difficult to stay upright. She leaned gently on the shoulder of her older brother, Sven, whose expression was grim but determined.

Augusta Larson

The siblings had been raised in a large family of devout Lutherans on a farm in Kalmar County on Sweden's south coast; they had very little money and food was always scarce. Born in 1864, Augusta was taught to sew by her mother Inga at an early age and, by the time she was seven, she was so skilled with a needle that she took charge not only of her family's mending, but the neighbors' mending, too, enabling her to make a significant contribution to the family finances.

Augusta's childhood was shadowed by the worst famine in Sweden's history. At the age of twelve, her parents considered sending her away to a sewing school, but Augusta argued vociferously against it and she continued to attend the local school, paying her way by making clothes for everyone in the area.

Augusta secretly harbored a dream to visit her half-siblings, who lived in the United States, in upstate New York. Between 1880 and 1890, about 325,000

Swedes emigrated to America. Some were fleeing social, political, and religious problems, but the majority were farmers, loggers, miners, and factory workers, motivated by economic hardship.

When Sven came across an ad from a Scandinavian steamship line encouraging young men like him to head west, Augusta jumped at the chance to accompany him on the crossing.

When Augusta at last reached the front of the line at Castle Garden, the immigration officer made an error in her arrival record: her last name was given as Lawson, a spelling she kept because it sounded more American.

Papers processed, Sven bought them both a train ticket from a booth inside the passenger ship terminal; he was worldly enough not to be conned into a more expensive ticket by the hustlers hanging around outside, hoping to prey on the innocent.

The pair headed to upstate New York, but within weeks Sven contracted typhoid fever and died.

What was Augusta to do?

She hated the idea of leaving Sven buried alone in a foreign country. She was also appalled by the prospect of undertaking another long sea voyage; she had only barely regained her strength after the first one.

She decided to stay in America.

As an unmarried woman in a strange land who spoke limited English, this adventure was never going to be easy. At first, she stayed with her half-sister and half-brother, Karolina Anderson and Rheinholt Larson, in Lakewood in upstate New York, working as a domestic in nearby Jamestown. After a couple of years, her exceptional skills as a seamstress got her a better paid job in a dressmaker's shop.

In 1888, Augusta packed her bags and headed for Chicago, where there was a huge Scandinavian immigrant population. She sensed there would be more opportunities for her there—not least, more opportunities to meet single, young men.

She settled in Evanston and found employment as a domestic servant, one of the more respectable jobs for a female immigrant. But life in Chicago proved as much a struggle as it had in New York, and it became clear that her best hope was to marry.

In 1892, when she spotted a "Wife Wanted" ad in a newspaper, she saw an opportunity.

The ad had been placed by Ole Ruud. Ole was born in 1847 on a small farm just outside Oslo in Norway. Life there was tough: in a later letter to his mother, he explained that "The narrow surroundings and my roaming disposition brought upon me the 'American Fever.'" In 1879, he set sail for America.

Ole Ruud

Ole became one of the earliest pioneers of Washington State, ploughing the semi-arid land and planting potatoes and wheat. He acquired a 160-acre homestead at the foot of Badger Mountain and was elected the first surveyor of Douglas County.

Soon after he turned forty-five, Ole decided it was time to find a wife. As women were scarce in Washington, matchmaking via the newspapers made a lot of sense.

Ole and Augusta wrote to each other for a few months. No doubt the fact that they were both immigrants from Scandinavia helped build a connection. And then on October 17, 1892, he mailed her enough money by registered letter to pay the fare 2,000 miles west to Washington. She took the train from Chicago to Spokane, then on to Coulee City, where the railroad line ended, continuing her journey by horse-drawn carriage across the grassy plains to Waterville, a pioneer town in the heart of the state.

Registry Receipt of letter to Augusta Larson containing fare to
Waterville, Washington, 1892

Main Street in Waterville, Washington, 1892

Augusta had little idea what awaited her. Like many female immigrants before her, she simply had to hope that the decision to throw her lot in with a man she had never met, in a state she had never visited, would eventually lead to a better life.

⸎

By 1870, one in four Americans lived in cities. The demographics of those who placed personal ads expanded to include factory workers and store clerks, and the first matrimonial journals, such as the *Matrimonial Times* and the *Matrimonial Herald*, were launched. Newspapers reached record numbers of readers due to expanded geographical range. The amount of money spent on advertising per year increased tenfold between 1865 and 1900; advertising for love was no exception, which is why it became more widespread during this period than at any other time until the Internet.

Take Chicago, where Ole Ruud placed his ad. In just two or three decades, the city had been transformed from a prairie trading post to a great metropolis. Its population doubled every year from 1850 to 1890, making it the nation's second largest city after New York. Many of the resources found west of the Mississippi ended up there: cattle were slaughtered by its meatpackers, pine forests processed by its lumber merchants, fresh produce traded by its entrepreneurs. A large proportion of the workforce were immigrants from Ireland, Germany, and Eastern Europe; in 1880, 42 percent of Chicago's residents were foreign-born, second only to San Francisco. While arranged marriages were still common in immigrant communities, the decision to seek a love match instead was a way of asserting a new, American identity, championing values like freedom and progress and rejecting the Old World in favor of the New.

Many Chicagoans, however, needed help finding a date in this increasingly urban, impersonal society, and the city's newspapers were happy to step in, beginning with the *Chicago Inter Ocean* and followed by the *Chicago Daily Tribune*, which by the 1870s featured four or five marriage ads a day. The men who advertised were a varied bunch: they included "a young physician, well educated, ambitious, with a little capital," "a successful young lawyer in the Far West," "a widower of 30, a mechanic," and "a young gentleman of large physique, temperate habits, holds an excellent position." It is notable how many boast of their sobriety: with the passing in 1851 of the Maine Law, one of the first laws to ban the sale of alcohol, the temperance movement was quickly gaining credence. Descriptions of the type of bride sought included "a lady of settled mind (Protestant) who loves to live according to the Lord's precepts," "an industrious, amiable and sensible young lady who would be willing to migrate Westward," and "a young widow of good education and pleasing address who can play the piano and sing; brunette preferred."

What sort of women answered these ads? In 1884, shortly after Grover Cleveland was elected president by a margin of just 23,000 votes, despite reports that as a young man he had fathered an illegitimate child, a reporter for the *Chicago Tribune* placed an ad in the guise of a rich Western rancher. He found that, contrary to his preconception that those who replied would be either schoolgirls having a lark or sex workers wanting business, most proved to be entirely respectable women genuinely looking for a husband. One reply was "written on the finest and most stylish rough white paper . . . The hand-writing is easy and . . . every letter and word indicates an educated woman. The spelling, grammar, and punctuation are faultless." When they met up, he found her to be "lady-like . . . beautiful and well-bred [with] fine eyes and dark hair . . . and she wore her clothes like a princess."

Many women placed their own ads in Chicago-area newspapers. A sample from 1880 includes "a German lady of 22," "an American lady, 20 years of age, anxious for a home of her own so she can give her little girl a good education," and many, many widows. They variously seek "a temperate and industrious husband, with a good trade and permanent income," "a cultivated gentleman," and "an honourable gentleman that could give her a good home; one high up in the Masonic order preferred."

Other cities in the Midwest soon followed Chicago's lead, most enthusiasti-cally Cincinnati: the *Cincinnati Enquirer* featured hundreds of ads throughout the 1870s and 1880s. With the introduction of the steamboat, Cincinnati's location at the center of the Corn Belt proved key to the distribution of pro-duce to New Orleans and the eastern seaboard. By the 1820s, it was known as "Porkopolis" because it processed more pigs than anywhere in the country. Out of the slaughterhouses came all sorts of new industries—soap, glue, leather, brushes—employing about 20,000 workers, many of whom needed a little assistance with the courtship process.

One of the earliest marriage ads in the *Cincinnati Enquirer* appeared in 1869 in between an ad for R. Walker & Co, Dyers and Gents' Clothing Renovators and an ad wanting to buy ten to twenty thousand old bricks. It read simply, "Correspondence with a limited number of young ladies; object, matrimony; no joke." Over the next decade, most editions carried between ten and twenty marriage ads a day from doctors, businessmen, even ministers, and also lots of women. They reveal a distinct shift in tone and content from ads in previous decades.

Cincinnati Enquirer, *April 12, 1869*

The period saw a new phrase, "object: matrimony," come into common use. Certainly, the majority of the men and women who advertised in the

Cincinnati Enquirer specifically sought marriage and therefore were keen to be clear and explicit in their intentions. But marriage was no longer the sole goal of a personal ad. The phrase "object: matrimony" was joined by the likes of "object: fun and pleasure," "object: fun and pastime," "object: fun and improvement," "object: fun and fortune," or even simply "object: fun." This more casual approach to relationships was revolutionary in its own way and posed an alarming threat to respectable society's moral code.

Most of these sorts of ads were from men, but there were a few from women, too, declaring "object: fun," "object: fun, love and the consequences," or "object: fun and perhaps matrimony." Some remained vague: "Wanted. The acquaintance of a gentleman." By 1872, it was apparently acceptable to place the following in the *Cincinnati Enquirer*: "A young lady of 20 would like the acquaintance of a nice middle-aged gentleman of means; object, pleasure during the summer months." The word "pleasure" can of course have many implications, but it jolts the reader nonetheless. One woman is particularly bold: "A gay and festive young lady, a stranger in the city, wishes to make the acquaintance of the handsomest young gentleman in Cincinnati. Address Isola, this office." (This was printed next to an ad that declares with a terrifying casualness, "Anyone wishing to adopt a baby girl, three months old, will please address Mrs. R at this office.")

Members of the urban working class began to make regular appearances in the personal columns for the first time. In 1873, a "young mechanic, 26 years old" declared that he "would like to correspond with an intelligent American lady, between the ages of 20 and 26; object matrimony." About 15 percent of the female population was employed at the time, so he was sensible to keep an open mind and thereby increase his chances of finding a date.

Also new to the lexicon were the first explicit references to body type, for example the *Cincinnati Enquirer* ad in 1881 from "A very fleshy gentleman with means wishes the acquaintance of a lady in like conditions and not over 30 years." This was perhaps the only era in American history when it was fashionable to be large. According to one tourist, young wealthy women were terrified of getting thin: "They are constantly having themselves weighed and every ounce of increase is hailed with delight." The voluptuous Lillian Russell was considered the great beauty of the Gilded Age and reporters gleefully covered her participation in contests to eat the most corn on the cob; one time, she revealed to the press that she had left her corset with the restaurant owner for safekeeping.

The increasingly modern outlook and tone of late-19th-century personal ads reflected a society in rapid transition. The period saw the invention of the typewriter, the telegram, and the telephone. In 1879 Thomas Edison patented the incandescent carbon-filament lamp, leading the way toward the large-scale introduction of electric light. Railroad mileage increased from 30,000 in 1860 to 193,000 in 1900. The world's first skyscraper, Chicago's Home Insurance Building, was erected in 1885. Department stores and mail-order business flourished and, at home, so did canned food and the gramophone. Meanwhile, the divorce rate increased nationally by 70 percent between 1880 and 1890, with two-thirds of suits filed by women. This was encouraged in part by the increasing liberalization of divorce laws; in most states, habitual drunkenness became grounds for divorce for the first time, while cruelty came to be defined far more loosely than in previous decades.

The Midwestern city of St. Louis was a relatively early adopter of personal ads; by 1879, the *St. Louis Post-Dispatch* was featuring at least a couple a day. Some wonderfully evoke the period, for example one from a widower in search of "a plain and practical young widow who would enjoy buggy rides, steamboat excursions and other pastimes." Most of the male advertisers were the usual suspects—a merchant, a retired doctor, a miller and grain dealer, a stock dealer, a gentleman in the drug business, a head clerk in a dry goods house—but the female advertisers are more idiosyncratic, for example the "Progressive lady of culture, a student of human nature, medicine and phrenology, 42 years of age, wants to correspond with a congenial companion, 45 to 50 years of age. Address Mrs. Grace Matrimony, this office, for two weeks." As the *St. Louis Globe-Democrat* commented in 1885, "For many men and women, the 'personal' columns of a newspaper have a strong attraction and in some cases have even brought about a desirable change in human fortune . . . a great many strong friendships, and even marriages are brought about by the answering of newspaper 'personals.'"

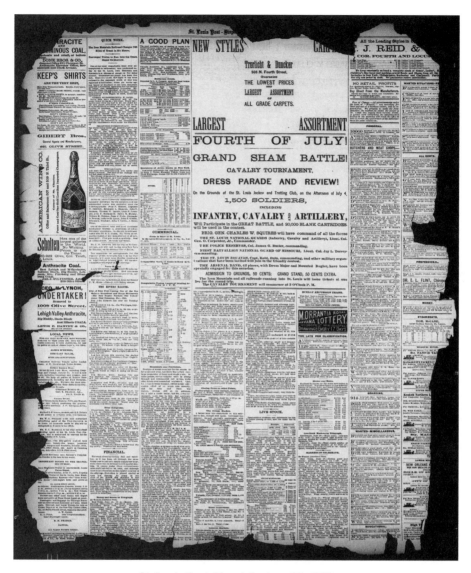

St. Louis Post-Dispatch, *June 28, 1879*

Although Chicago, Cincinnati, and St. Louis demonstrated perhaps the most enthusiasm for personal ads, by the end of the 19th century they had become a regular feature of almost every big city newspaper, with the largest numbers to be found in the *Charleston Daily News* in South Carolina ("A young farmer desires the acquaintance of a active young lady. Object, matrimony"), the *Saint Paul Globe* in Minnesota ("A young American gentleman, lately from the East, is desirous of forming the acquaintance of a young American lady of education, refinement, and good financial standing . . ."), and the *Indianapolis News* in Indiana ("A gentleman 30 years of age, formerly Major in the United States army and Colonel in the Spanish and Mexican armies, desires to correspond with a young lady between the age of 18 and 20 . . .").

By 1900, the country boasted 2,190 daily newspapers and 15,813 weekly newspapers, more than the rest of the world combined. Many carried personal ads, and widely publicized happily-ever-after stories helped boost the ads' popularity even further. In 1896, eighty-year-old John T. Hutchinson of Marietta, Ohio, replied to a "Husband Wanted" ad placed by Georgiana Allen, the wealthy seventy-year-old widow of a Florida politician. They met for the first time on the train platform: she inspected him at length and declared, "You'll do." The couple headed directly to the courthouse where they were married at eight o'clock that night. "Although very old," commented the reporter, "they are seemingly as frisky as young folks."

Marriage had become a highly marketable commodity.

One morning in 1873, a lawyer named Peter Patterson went to see his doctor complaining of headaches, stomach pain, and depression. "I couldn't relish my coffee this morning; I left my milk toast untouched," he said. "Hateful life, that of a bachelor at a hotel." The doctor suggested he place an ad for a wife in the *Matrimonial News*.

The *Matrimonial News* had been founded just two years previously as America's first newspaper dedicated solely to marriage ads. Billed as "a weekly journal devoted to the promotion of marriage and conjugal felicity," it had offices in San Francisco and Kansas City but was on sale all across the country. Each weekly issue carried three to four hundred ads; men paid twenty-five cents to place one, but for women there was no charge. "[I]n this day of travel," it noted, "when men and women leave home and acquaintances in search of wealth and happiness, the need of some method of honorable introduction between the sexes . . . is felt by all strangers in a strange place."

Patterson took his doctor's advice. His ad in the *Matrimonial News* was spotted by a forty-year-old widow named Louise Muntle, who lived on a farm in Kansas. She invited Patterson to visit, recording her first impression in her diary: "Nice fellow, solid, plenty of money; thinks himself ill, but isn't; ought to be married; told him so, but he hates the idea of courting." They wed, and after eight weeks on a diet of homemade bread, fresh strawberries, and herb tea, Patterson made a full recovery.

With happy endings like this, no wonder the *Matrimonial News* was soon joined by competitors like the *Matrimonial Reporter,* the *Matrimonial Advocate,* and the *Marriage Gazette,* all of which were popular throughout the 1870s and 1880s. The loosening of traditional social bonds had created a demand for new methods of matchmaking which, when met with the kind of entrepreneurial spirit that informed much of late 19th-century life, resulted in a number of new business opportunities. As the *Matrimonial Reporter* noted:

> Civilization, combined with the cold formalities of society and the rules of etiquette, imposed such restrictions on the sexes that there are thousands of marriageable men and women of all ages capable of making each other happy, who never have a chance of meeting . . . Therefore, the desirability of having some organ through which ladies and gentlemen aspiring to marriage can be honorably brought into communication, is too obvious to need a demonstration.

Every edition contained hundreds of ads, alongside lively advice columns about how to write a love letter or what makes a successful marriage.

These matrimonial newspapers catered to a broader customer base than the personals columns of mainstream newspapers. Take nineteen-year-old Maudie, for whom it was almost certainly the first time she had ever seen herself in print when she opened up a Kansas City edition of the *Matrimonial Times* in 1877 to admire the ad she had placed: a "jolly little girl of 17, with black hair and eyes and fair complexion, 115 pounds" was looking for a man who was "not stout, brown hair and mustache." Maudie was one of the tens of thousands of young people who abandoned the rural West during the farm crises of the 1870s, when the price of many staple crops collapsed, mainly due to an increase in production worldwide. Wheat went from $1.45 a bushel in 1866 to 49 cents a bushel in 1894, while corn and cotton followed a similar pattern. Agrarian debt increased hugely and many farms were forced to take on a mortgage to survive.

Thirty farm girls fled in search of work for every one farm boy who did. The result was a dramatic reversal in the traditional pattern of Western settlement: in urban areas, there were suddenly far more single migrant women than men. Reformer Mary Livermore traveled the country giving speeches that urged parents to teach their daughters to be self-sufficient because the chance of them getting married was dwindling fast: men, she said, were dying in great numbers from overwork or debauchery, while those who survived were mostly lazy or sick.

Predictably, the more personal ads that appeared, the more criticism they received. "Advertising for a wife is about as absurd as getting measured for an umbrella," opined Artemus Ward, generally considered America's first stand-up comedian, in 1862. "It is absurd—it is mean—and I suspect that most of those fellows who adopt that method of securing domestic bliss ought to hammer stone in some well-regulated penitentiary." A journalist in 1870 ranted about "these vile sink-holes of all corruption through which so many thousands of the young of both sexes in our midst disappear from happiness and respectability year after year!" Similarly, when the *Elyria Independent* in Ohio was sent a promotional copy of the recently launched *Matrimonial Bazar* in 1875, its editor opined that "While there are some sharp, cute things in this *Bazar*, its contents as a whole are simply disgusting . . ."

The worry was that personal ads represented a threat to the social order. They turned marriage into just another business transaction, and also broke down class barriers by allowing everyone and anyone to appear together in the same public forum. Many were concerned about the broader impact of people from wildly different backgrounds meeting and marrying each other. A lawyer and a farm girl, for instance? Unthinkable! As historian of marriage Nancy Cott has argued, "If marriage produced the polity, then wrongfully joined marriages could be fatal. The presence of such marriages and their perpetrators might infect the whole body politic."

Yet personal ads continued to flourish.

⋙

On November 24, 1892, just five weeks after Augusta Larson arrived in Waterville, Washington, she married Ole Ruud in a small service at the local Lutheran church. She was twenty-eight, he was forty-three. Their first child was born almost exactly nine months later.

The life Augusta and Ole built together was the very definition of a pioneer existence. Hardship was the norm. "I have worked very hard this past winter when I had to go out in deep snow to feed the cattle and milk our four cows, in addition to all my other work," Augusta wrote in a letter back home. The couple had three daughters and five sons together. But after 1908, when their daughter Signe died of appendicitis, Augusta often clung to a formaldehyde-filled bottle she kept hidden in the corner of a closet. It contained her daughter's appendix.

Their other children prospered, though. One daughter married an executive at the American Canning Company in San Francisco, another married his brother, while a son fell for one of the first women graduates of the University of Washington.

Ole and Augusta died in California, where they had moved to be closer to their children once they became too old to farm. These emblematic pioneers of the Pacific Northwest would likely never have met had Augusta not happened to stumble across Ole's personal ad while drinking her tea one Sunday morning on the balcony of a scruffy tenement building on Chicago's east side.

Betty

St. Louis, 1900

I didn't mean to cheat the men at first. It just seemed like a lark.

A friend at work, Alice, put me up to it—I blame her. As she said, what was the difference, really, between a man taking you to see a show and buying you a drink and a man sending you a necklace and $20 for a rail fare?

I did feel rather envious of Alice's new leather boots with the tiny buttons down the side. Hers were green, but I wondered about getting red for myself.

I also wanted my own copy of that book The Wonderful Wizard of Oz *by Frank someone. All the girls in the office were reading it.*

Most of all, I was worried about how I was going to pay my rent. The woman who ran my boardinghouse had seemed so motherly at first, but she soon turned her mouth on me when the money didn't turn up when she wanted it.

And so, I decided to place an advertisement. Or rather, an English duchess with a castle to inherit and $50,000 a year decided to place an advertisement.

CHAPTER NINE

"A Discreet Young Lady":
A Turn-of-the-Century
Crime Wave, c. 1900

H e got foxy and I froze him out."
This was what Lulu Raines told police in 1898 when she was arrested
for swindling hundreds of dollars out of a credulous suitor.

Raines had placed ads in small-town newspapers all over Texas looking for "a
loving, kind, husband," adding that "I am not looking for a rich man. I prefer
a poor one. Wish to marry soon." The resulting replies allowed her to amass
$7,000 in cash and $3,000 in jewelry in just six months. Among the victims was
soldier Philip Housan, garrisoned at Fort Walla Walla in Washington, whom
Raines told a local reporter "sent me a diamond bracelet, four diamond rings,
and a set of fine earrings, and was so impressed that he sent his mother and sister
to visit me." Call it an example of female empowerment.

Raines was by no means the only opportunist to spot the criminal potential
of advertising for love. This was *the* era of the "confidence man," or con man,
a term coined mid-century that quickly earned itself the lengthiest entry in
the *National Police Gazette*'s *Rogue's Lexicon*. Herman Melville's last published
book, *The Confidence-Man* (1857), was about a stranger who sneaks aboard a

Mississippi riverboat on April Fool's Day intent on tricking its passengers. Across the nation, scams were commonplace—nowhere more so than in the big cities like New York.

In the 1890s, the *New York Times* featured an average of a story a week of personal ads gone awry, each one sadder and more bizarre than the last. Initially, the most common tale was a woman tricked out of her life savings. Take the One-Armed Bigamist, a nickname the paper bestowed upon one James C. Taylor in 1893. Taylor answered an ad in a New York newspaper from a widow named Mrs. Marie H. Leroy. They were married before the week was out and immediately headed to Niagara Falls for a honeymoon. After persuading her to withdraw her entire life savings—$850—from the bank and give it to him for "safe-keeping," he absconded the next morning. This was not the first time the One-Armed Bigamist had struck, and the state of New York eventually sentenced him to three years in jail.

For some, this sort of scam proved to be their first foray into a life of crime. In 1893, Carl Mueller conspired with a gang of fellow German immigrants to place ads aimed at farmers in the West, persuading them to send small sums of money in the hope of finding a wife. He was jailed for a year for postal fraud, but while locked up he hatched an even more wicked plan with his cellmate, the soon-to-be-notorious Dr. Henry Meyer. Mueller would entice women to marry him, take out an insurance policy on their life, then Meyer would poison them with arsenic and they would split the proceeds. It backfired when Mueller quite liked one of his wives and decided to testify against his former partner, who was convicted of second-degree murder and given a life sentence.

Then there were the bigamists. In 1905, a woman with the spectacular name of Mrs. May Gildersleeve obtained a decree of separation and alimony of $10 a week by proving that her husband, Dr. Walter H. Maynard, whom she had met through an ad, was already married to two other women.

Where New York leads, others follow. Newspapers across the nation gleefully reported tale after tale of crimes perpetrated through the personals: theft, fraud, bigamy, and even murder. There were almost certainly a few repeat offenders, but police departments did not routinely exchange information, there was no nationwide method of cataloguing crimes, and fingerprinting was not introduced until the St. Louis World's Fair in 1904. As a result, nobody put the pieces of the puzzle together to determine the scope of this crime wave.

In 1889, newspapers entertained their readers with the scandalous tale of Seymour Hitchcock. Hitchcock was the son of a well-to-do farmer in Franklin, Pennsylvania. While still living with his parents, he spotted an ad in the newspaper from Sarah Hugell, whom he swiftly married. At first the newlyweds sponged off his exasperated father, but when he kicked them out they moved to Oneonta in the Catskills: there, they could be completely anonymous, and it also had the advantage of being an easy ride from Pennsylvania on the recently built Delaware and Hudson Railway.

In Oneonta, the couple came up with a new scheme to make a buck. They placed ads in various Chicago newspapers to the effect that "a respectable young widow" wanted to meet a "Western gentleman of means and good standing, with a view to matrimony." Those who replied received a letter containing a photograph of a beautiful young woman and a request for an expensive present to demonstrate the depth of their ardor, or for the money for the train fare so that they could meet.

The records of the Oneonta post office show that, in just eight weeks, the Hitchcocks swindled over $400 out of several gullible, single men in the form of money orders, letters containing cash, and parcels of jewelry. When Sarah was arrested, she blamed her husband for leading her astray and managed to escape prosecution; Seymour, however, went to jail.

Chicago was the ideal place to carry out a scam: a crowded metropolis, many of whose residents were new in town and desperate.

> When Caroline Meeber boarded the afternoon train for Chicago, her total outfit consisted of a small trunk, a cheap imitation alligator skin satchel holding some minor details of the toilet, a small lunch in a paper box and a yellow snap purse, contained her ticket, a scrap of paper with her sister's address in Van Buren Street, and four dollars in money. It was August, 1889. She was eighteen years of age, bright, timid, and full of the illusions of ignorance and youth.

This is the opening scene of Theodore Dreiser's novel *Sister Carrie* (1900), whose realism was widely considered revolutionary. Arriving in Chicago, determined to escape her small-town existence, Carrie is unable to find a job. At first she thinks her best route to financial security is to hitch her lot to a man, but after being swindled by various suitors, she becomes a successful actress; this was one of the few career opportunities open to women, but it meant losing one's entrée to polite society.

It was a narrative with which many of Dreiser's readers could surely empathize. In 1886, under the attention-grabbing headline, "How a Chicago Scoundrel Enticed a Susceptible Young Teacher from her School," newspapers all over the Midwest reported on the case of Jennie E. Sheeley, "an almost friendless school-teacher in one of the small towns in the interior of Dakota," who was spotted by a friendly (some might say nosy) policeman wandering around a Chicago train depot, trying to find a hotel where she had arranged to meet a man with whom she had been corresponding after answering his personal ad.

Scams were also rife in St. Louis, where Charles Hocking was arrested in 1895 for conning dozens of women out of their savings. Hocking would answer a marriage ad, arrange the wedding as quickly as possible, ask the new wife to invest in his business, then skip town. He was only caught when one of his victims decided to seek revenge. She advertised for a husband a second time, but under a different name. She and Hocking arranged to meet, but when he arrived (according to the local newspaper), "she flogged him with a heavy whip until she was tired, and with his face and neck cut he escaped through a rear door, scaled a fence and disappeared."

A large number of matrimonial agencies were founded in this period. Some were dedicated to helping single men and women partner up, but the majority were on the make. They would place ads in newspapers all over the country, usually from men or women who sounded too good to be true: a widow worth $50,000 or a handsome, wealthy businessman. The giveaway was that every ad directed letters to be sent to the same address, usually in Chicago or New York, which on investigation turned out to be the office building where the agency was based.

Oscar Wells was arrested five times between 1902 and 1905 in various Midwestern cities for setting up a series of fraudulent matrimonial agencies, attracting clients with ads like, "Young widow without kith or kin, but a lover of home and children, is worth in cash and city property at least $80,000, left her by a deceased husband." He then promised introductions to nonexistent wealthy men and women in exchange for a $5 membership fee. When police raided his Chicago office, they found an estimated 45,000 letters from would-be clients.

Wells's defense was that he was just making the most of the situation. As the desire to marry, and marry rich, was felt particularly powerfully during the Gilded Age, many Midwesterners proved to be a vulnerable combination of gullible and greedy. According to the judge sentencing Wells, "To sell women and men in marriage is the height of crime." This seems a little harsh, but it reflected a continuing widespread anxiety that every aspect of modern life was becoming distastefully commercialized. Most newspaper commentators seemed to suggest it served the victims right. Wells only got caught when a high-profile Chicago detective, Clifton R. Wooldridge, took it upon himself to raid a number of matrimonial agencies.

Wooldridge also brought down Marion Grey, a glamorous twenty-year-old, college-educated woman from a small town called Benton Harbor in Michigan. Blessed with an entrepreneurial spirit, Grey set up a matrimonial agency in the suburbs of Chicago called the Searchlight Matrimonial Club. By advertising that she had wealthy clients on her books looking for husbands and wives, she managed to accumulate over $3,000 in five-dollar membership fees in just three months. Grey's assistant testified that they had sent the same photograph of a beautiful Kansas City actress, Cora Cline, to hundreds of members.

Grey was put on trial for fraud, but the case quickly acquired broader significance. The assistant district attorney argued in his closing statement that, "The sacred institution of marriage is involved in this case . . . Can love matches be made by a paltry $5 policy in an affinity agency? If you permit the operation of this kind of business it will undermine society, break up our homes, and place our wives and daughters in danger." He went on, "It is a disgrace to civilization—this worldwide hunting of affinities and soulmates." The judge criticized Grey for her "mercenary matchmaking" and sentenced her to a year in prison, but President Taft commuted her sentence and she only served a month. It was unusual to face jail time for a crime of this sort—a fine was more common—but female con artists were always judged more harshly than male ones. Perhaps the authorities also intended to make an example of Grey in an attempt to restore some respectability to the courtship process.

Marion Grey

The personals in the *New York Herald* were implicated in the most high-profile scandal of all. By the turn of the century, they took up almost all of the paper's front page; a popular form of entertainment, they were also, in some ways, a form of urban newsgathering, like gossiping over the garden fence. The advertising magazine *Printers' Ink* called the *Herald*'s personal column "one of the most attractive and alluring that appears in any paper anywhere," while the *New York American* claimed it brought in a profit of over $200,000 a year.

Over time the personals in the *Herald* had become determinedly risqué, variously offering sex ("Gentleman, disengaged, offers confidential services to large, stylish lady or widow of means") or seeking money ("Will wealthy gentleman befriend English young lady; refined, educated, lonely?") or sometimes both. Depending on one's point of view, this represented either the downfall of society or a welcome opportunity for women to empower themselves sexually and/or financially.

In the strict moral climate of turn-of-the-century America, this state of affairs could not last. In 1906, newspaper mogul William Randolph Hearst instructed reporters for the *New York American* to investigate the personals columns of the rival *Herald*. Hearst wanted revenge for a recent failed gubernatorial campaign which he in part blamed on the negative editorials printed by the *Herald*'s proprietor, James Gordon Bennett Jr. What he got was a shocking exposé of the world of personal ads.

According to a female reporter for the *American*, some of the ads placed by men "made it quite clear that they wanted a good time and not a helpmeet. All sections of the city and all walks of life seemed to be represented in the advertisers," the implication being that this democratic approach to the page was to be treated as a cause for concern. When the reporter took it upon herself to reply to some of the ads, the letters she received were indeed rather racy. Enquiring of one what exactly he wanted from her, he wrote "Your note at hand. I am ashamed to tell you what I want. I must whisper it in your ear. Can I?" Another described himself to her as a man with "broad ideas." The problem was that it was almost impossible to vet the advertiser: apart from the content of the ad itself, the exchange of a few letters, and gut feeling, there was nothing else to go on. And therein lay the danger, especially for women.

Some of the personals appeared alongside ads for massage parlors, which the *American* also undertook to investigate. When a reporter visited a woman advertising massages out of her apartment, he found that "The only furniture in the room was a raised cot, a stand on which there were three boxes of talcum powder, and a basin of water . . . The details of the massage which the woman practiced are not printable."

Another reporter explained that some women came to New York with the specific intent of finding a "gentleman protector" and "if their own statements are to believed they know of the *Herald* and turn to it at once." The result was ads full of euphemisms, for example: "A discreet young lady, cosy home, appreciates meeting generous gentleman; matrimony." The reference to matrimony was an attempt to appear respectable, at least at quick glance. According to one advertiser, "they won't take the ad at the *Herald* unless you put that in . . . I've talked it over with the clerks there, and they say it's necessary to keep from violating the law. They know I don't want to marry, and most of those who answer know it, too."

Many of the women who advertised were migrants from outside the city; a reporter spoke to one who had grown up on a farm in eastern Pennsylvania but now found herself living in a New York garret so small it could only fit a bed, trunk, dresser, and chair. She explained that, "I am employed as a telephone girl by the Crane Company in the St. James Building at Broadway and Twenty-sixth Street . . . and as I only get $6 a week and have to pay $3 for this room I need financial assistance and must entertain men." The *Herald* was accused of promoting vice, prostitution, and even the white slave trade, but what the *American*'s investigation really revealed were the limited options available to women without independent means.

But let us not pity all these women. The number of working women increased from two million in 1870 to eight million in 1910, causing a generational shift in women's expectations of what courtship entailed. Many rebelled against the traditional rules of Victorian heterosexual courtship, which dictated that it always took place in private and with marriage the goal; instead, an evening out with a male companion in a public space like a restaurant or a theater, with him picking up the bill, was sometimes an economic exchange that suited them. A changing moral code, accompanied by a growing clamor for women's self-determination, made this a not-quite-but-nearly-respectable option for the very first time.

Nevertheless, in 1906, the *Herald* was indicted for sending obscenity through the mail and fined $31,000. Its reputation never fully recovered from the scandal.

It was only a matter of time before those with a murderous tendency spotted the potential of the personals. In 1904, Johann Hoch placed an ad in the *Abendpost*, a popular German-language newspaper based in Chicago.

> Matrimony. Widow without children, under the 30's, German, own home, acquaintance of a lady, object—matrimony. Address M422 Abendpost. Respectfully J. Hoch, 6430 Union Avenue, City.

A reply soon arrived from forty-five-year-old Marie Schippnik Walcker. Originally from Hamburg, Germany, Walcker had recently gotten divorced, using the money she made from doing other people's laundry to open a candy story on the corner of Willow and Larrabee on Chicago's north side. It proved a struggle to turn a profit, though, and she was soon keen to find someone with whom to share the burden.

As soon as Hoch received Marie's letter, he jumped on one of Chicago's newly built streetcars to go and visit. When he arrived at her house, he was shown into the parlor at the back, where he spun her a tale about how he used to have a wife and four children but they had all died before he was able to spend his nest egg of $8,000 on them. After they had chatted for a while, Hoch asked Marie outright if she liked him.

"Why, Mr. Hoch, of course I do," Marie replied.

"Well, you like me and I like you, so we can get married, eh?"

That same night, Hoch sat down at his desk, opened his notebook, and calculated the cost of the wicked plan he had hatched for his soon-to-be bride.

FUNERAL EXPENSES.
Coffin $45
Shroud $7
Carriages (3) $15
Hearse $7
Total $94
(Gravedigger ?
Hat $5)

To include a new hat in your calculations of the cost of your future wife's funeral is quite something.

They were married three days later. Marie fell ill within weeks: her first symptom was her complexion turning an alarming shade of yellow, which was due to the arsenic her husband was regularly mixing in with her food, leading to kidney and liver failure. It turned out that this was a tactic Hoch had used many times before.

Johann Hoch

Hoch was eventually found guilty of Marie's murder and sentenced to death. He was suspected of murdering a further fifty women or so in total, but this was never proved. The newspapers dubbed him "Bluebeard," while an alderman for the North Side bemoaned how "In a decade, the city of which we are so proud has gone through a woeful change . . . Chicago [is] a city of lawlessness and of our civic shame." On the day of Hoch's hanging, the *American* devoted two hundred and fifty column inches to the story, compared to just twenty columns in the *Chicago Tribune*. It is thanks to the *American*'s sensationalist coverage, accompanied by splashy pictures and eye-catching headlines, that we know so much about him.

The many other cases of murder perpetrated through the personals in this period did not receive nearly so much attention. To take one example among dozens, late at night on October 9, 1907, the body of a young woman named Grace Albin was found washed ashore at Shippan Point in Stamford, Connecticut. She was dressed in a black coat and a white shirtwaist; in her pocket was a clipping of a matrimonial ad from a woman closely matching her description. When the *New York Times* followed up, it found that she had recently left her husband and was working on a barge traveling between New York and New London. Other than this one small story, however, Grace Albin's life and death went entirely unnoticed elsewhere in the press. It was a sad end to a sad life.

The Gilded Age was not gilded for everyone. Millions struggled with financial hardship, in particular women. Pensions or personal investment plans did not exist and the government offered little help. Others were able to support themselves but simply did not want to toil through life alone. The very premise of the personals—anonymity—made them especially attractive to scam artists. Increased geographical mobility, along with a lack of community ties, meant that weeks could pass by before family and friends back home realized one of their loved ones was missing. A large proportion of the victims were recently arrived immigrants, fearful of living alone in this bewildering new social order and highly vulnerable to mistreatment by those claiming to offer financial security. Just like Internet scams today, it was those most desperate to escape their existing circumstances who were the most easily conned. While personal ads could bring enormous happiness, they also, increasingly with their popularity, carried enormous risk.

Edward

Arizona, 1905

"Stop crying, Daddy!" My youngest used to shout that at me all the time, but when my oldest started saying it too, I realized I probably ought to make a change.

My six children were fed, clothed, and had somewhere to sleep at night, but they sure weren't happy.

Their mother had died the night after I completed the purchase of the mine. Suddenly I had two hundred men working for me and all the money in the world, but the light had gone from my life.

It wasn't just the children who needed a woman around. I missed having a best friend. My foreman tried his best, but he smelt too strongly of stinkdamp.

But how to find her? This was no life for a city girl keen on rummy and ribbons, and the only local women round these parts were old marrieds or Indians.

In my favor, though, was the railroad, which had just reached us. Maybe this would bring me my savior? I heard the steam train chugging into town every night as I sat at my kitchen table drinking too much when I should have been going to bed.

And so, I decided to place an advertisement.

CHAPTER TEN

"No Old Maids or Fast Widows": The Western Frontier, c. 1900

T wo hundred wives wanted.

This plea appeared in newspaper ads all over the West in 1906. They had been placed by the men of Big Horn County in Wyoming, one of the last frontier areas in the United States to be settled due to its extremely remote location. The list of eligible bachelors included a stockman named D. H. Ralston worth $1,000,000, a sheep man named James Dickie worth $500,000, and a postmaster named E. C. Blonde worth $400,000—or so they claimed.

E. C. Blonde, known to his friends and family as Charles, was born in Massachusetts in 1866 to French parents. At the age of twenty-three, he left home to seek his fortune and before long found himself working for the Department of the Interior as chief herder in Shoshoni, Wyoming, for $75 a month. He was later appointed postmaster of Big Horn County, a job he enjoyed but for the almost entire absence of women from the region.

His marriage ad received a huge number of replies. According to the local paper, "it is understood that several of the Denver girls who have answered the ads have secured positions, but the men are very quiet about taking Denver girls into the wilds of Wyoming, as they fear a protest on the part of Denver swains."

One of the women who spotted the ad was Ada Edwards, born in Missouri to Southern parents, who by 1906 was thirty-two, a schoolteacher, and living in an overcrowded boardinghouse in North Fork, Wyoming.

There was a huge demand for schoolteachers in pioneer country; Wyoming was one of the first states to forbid sex discrimination in the hiring of teachers, a law passed in part in a bid to increase female immigration. (For the same reason, in 1869 Wyoming became the first state to give women the right to vote.)

Ada and Charles embarked on a correspondence and within weeks she agreed to marry him. In 1909, they had twin boys, Frank and Chas. Ada stayed home to take care of them while Charles worked as a self-employed stock farmer. Charles's brother also lived with them, helping out on the farm.

The Blondes continued to prosper. In 1921, they moved to Alhambra, California, where the twins attended the local high school. Charles died in 1928; Ada lived in the house they had bought together, which was worth $5,000, until she died thirty years later, aged eighty-three.

The twins Frank and Chas stayed in California, where they both married, had families, and served honorably in World War II. Immediately after the war Frank took a job at a gas station, while Chas worked in a drug store; they both ended up as salesmen.

The geographical isolation experienced by Charles Blonde and many like him on the frontier meant that, sometimes, the only way to find a wife and start a family was via an ad. Despite this, the traditional historical narrative of the region has entirely ignored the crucial role played by the personals in redressing the prevailing gender imbalance. Tracing the lives of those like Ada and Charles who met this way helps explain how the West was populated, couple by couple, family by family. How America grew. How a nation was built.

∗

Wyoming was not the only region in the West to suffer from a chronic shortage of single women of marriageable age. It affected all the Mountain States: according to a survey of Idaho taken in the *Ladies' Home Journal* in 1899, there were 16,584 single men to 1,426 single women. The magazine declared the region "a heaven for spinsters and widows." A mining engineer in Irwin,

Colorado, noted in his diary that no fewer than forty men were courting the town's only respectable unmarried woman, the camp doctor's wife's sister. A system was set up limiting the parlor to six callers at a time; each got a maximum of "4 minutes on sofa with girl."

The traditional image of courtship in the West was that it was a hasty, spur-of-the-moment affair, but in truth most couples adhered to the same rituals played out in more settled areas: the man paid a formal call on the woman and her family at home, then, if this went smoothly, they pursued other opportunities to get to know each other in supervised environments such as dances and parties, church services and sporting events, lectures and clubs, and so on. The high rate of divorce in the West, however, suggests that the courtship process was not functioning as it should.

Happily, fluid cultural norms in the West liberated many of its young people to explore alternative matchmaking methods without the judgment and censure frequently experienced in more established societies. This also spoke to the streak of self-determination that was increasingly coming to define the Western identity.

The residents of the Mountain States turned to marriage ads as early as the 1860s. One in the *Miner* in 1867, reprinted by the *Montana Post*, read simply "Wanted—a wife, by a young, temperate and industrious miner. No old maids or fast widows need apply" [a "fast widow" referred to a woman who was already married but looking to trade up]. Ads were commonplace in Utah by the 1880s, for example in the *Salt Lake Herald* in 1881: "A young man with means, late from the east, is wishing to answer any young lady with good character, and respectable. Charles A. White, South Cottonwood, Utah."

Arizona embraced personal ads especially enthusiastically. Some placed them in local newspapers, like the lively ad in the *Arizona Sentinel* in 1875 for a "nice, plump, healthy, good-natured, good-looking, domesticated and affectionate lady" who "must be 22 to 35 years of age" and "a believer in God and immortality, but no sectarian. She must not be a gad-about or given to scandal, but must be one who will be a help-mate or companion, and who will endeavor to make home happy." Demands of this sort fit into a Western ethic that emphasized ideals of personal satisfaction, the search for happiness, the importance of the individual, and so on, but are also typical of the Victorian-era emphasis on the importance of romantic love when making marital decisions.

Some Arizonian singletons searched further afield, placing their ads in the *New York Herald*:

> GENTLEMAN OF 30, COLLEGE GRADUATE AND
> practical mining engineer, who has spent the last ten
> years in the Western Territories and mining regions, and
> is now the owner of valuable mines in Arizona which, if
> properly developed, will yield a large fortune within a
> few years, being alone in the world and without acquaint-
> ances in the East, desires to form the acquaintance of a
> highly respectable young lady of means, indcomdently
> situated, well educated and refined, and of amiable and
> sympathetic temperament, with a view to a prosperous
> business partnership, or marriage if mutually agreeable.
> Address, in strict confidence, C. F. SPAULDING, Herald
> office.

Others turned to matrimonial newspapers like the *Matrimonial News*, for example the "Three young men, in Prescott, Arizona" who described themselves as "Physician, age 30, merchant age 24 and wealthy mine-owner aged 33, all having plenty of filthy lucre." They continued, "Send true name, we mean business. Merchant, W.T. Rowe; physician, Dr. Warren E. Day; mine owner, Jay G. Kelley. Prescott, Yavapai Co., Arizona Ter." The ad dates from 1877; is it a coincidence that a wedding took place for at least one of these young men just three years later? Records show that Warren E. Day of Prescott, Arizona, married Mary M. Gilbert of Pennsylvania on March 1, 1880. Apparently, the "filthy lucre" worked!

The opening of the Santa Fe and Southern Pacific railroads in the 1880s massively increased transport links to Arizona, making it easier than ever to persuade single men and women from all over the states to take a chance on love. In 1885, six married women living in mining camps near Tucson set up what they called the Busy Bee Club in an effort to increase female African American immigration to the area. They ran ads in newspapers on the East Coast, which met with a fair amount of success and helped make the frontier more racially diverse. The fact that such ads were rare is also a depressing reminder of the way young single African American men and women were repeatedly excluded from both placing and replying to personal ads in this period.

The Pacific states were even more in need of a way to persuade women that eligible men eagerly awaited them. By 1852, 25,855 men, 7,021 women, and 8,270 children had passed through Fort Kearny, Nebraska, on their way to Oregon, revealing a wider demographic trend about those who made this intrepid journey: very few were women.

The dearth of women was not just a problem for the individuals involved, but also more broadly for the Oregon authorities. The 1850 Donation Land Act, intended to promote settlement in Oregon, gave 640 acres to every married couple who settled in the Oregon Territory before December 1 (double the 320 acres given to every unmarried white male). With this in mind, in 1859 a number of pleas were published in newspapers across the country to try to persuade women to immigrate: "Don't be backward but come right along, all you who want good husbands and comfortable homes, in the most beautiful country and finest climate of the world." The town of Albany went one step further in 1864, hiring two brothers named Benton to travel east for the same purpose. "Brides Wanted," proclaimed their flyers, painting an enticing picture of Oregon as "peaceful, tree-filled terrain, endless blue skies, and a husband for every widow and spinster." Astonishingly, they managed to recruit over a hundred women to go back to Oregon with them, but this proved only a short-term fix.

Ads were sporadically appearing in the *Oregon Argus* by the 1850s, for example from "a man in good circumstances, of an agreeable disposition, and who is engaged in a lucrative business" looking for a "single lady, of from twenty-five to thirty-five years of age, of fair personal appearance, and possessing good health, a good disposition, a tolerable education, and who is also economical." The Portland newspaper the *Morning Oregonian* carried marriage ads by the late 1860s; take the "respectable, well-to-do gentleman" who advertised under the excitable headline, "A Wife Wanted!"

Morning Oregonian, *February 10, 1869*

By the turn of the century, marriage ads were to be found in almost every edition of the *Morning Oregonian*. Here is a favorite from 1901:

> A farmer (Norwegian born), 39 years, single, sober and good worker, would like to meet a gentle, affectionate and respectable woman of about the same age, with a view to marriage. Prefer one that is content with farmer's life, not "stylish," but willing to become a good help-mate and rear a family in a substantial, happy way. I am not looking for beauty, but: a person of good health, affectionate and with some means is appreciated, and will in this way secure a true, loving husband. Answer by letter, with full information. P.O. Box 623, Portland, Or.

Sweet, right?

Some of the ads in the *Oregonian* sound too good to be true, and they probably are the work of one of the matrimonial agencies that sprang up to meet the increasing demands of isolated local men and women. For example: "A young lady, independently wealthy, jolly disposition, very musical, would correspond with kind-hearted gent of good habits, with marriage as a possibility." And for the fairer sex, there was this: "Gentleman, good reputation, wealthy and liberally disposed, worth $200,000, with beautiful home, seeks appreciative wife." It is absurd to imagine that a man with $200,000 at his disposal would truly have had trouble finding a match, unless he was the world's pickiest person. Further doubt is cast by the ad a few lines further down in the personals column: "Wanted—a young woman to give baths and massage. Call after noon, 131½ Fourth st."

Curiously, California's first personal ads were placed by women. Dorothy Scraggs appealed to the male population of Marysville in 1849 by describing herself as "a lady who can wash, cook, scour, sew, milk, spin, weave, hoe, (can't plow), cut wood, make fires, feed the pigs, raise chickens, rock the cradles . . ." Scraggs was acutely aware of her worth as an asset in this newly settled state. Meanwhile, in a San Francisco newspaper in 1851, "Julia" declared to the world that "Whereas my husband has left me without provocation on my part, I hereby advertise for a suitable person to fill the vacancy. The gentleman applying must have blue eyes, light moustache (my husband had black), an attractive goatee, and a genteel figure.

He must not be over twenty-five years of age, well-educated, of unexceptionable morals, and agreeable address. It is requisite that his personal incumbrances should be limited, and his prospective fortunes flattering. No gamblers need apply."

Following James W. Marshall's discovery of gold nuggets at a sawmill on the banks of the American River in the Sacramento Valley in early 1848, which resulted in the Gold Rush, men flocked to the West Coast in enormous numbers, leading to a greater gender disparity than anywhere else in the nation. The census of 1850 revealed the female population of California to be just 8 percent of the state's inhabitants (this figure failed to include either prostitutes or Native Americans, neither of who were generally viewed as wife material). In mining communities, the demographics were even more skewed: in Mariposa, for example, there were only 108 women out of a population of 4,379. The number of women increased slightly following the opening of the Panama Canal railway in 1850, but only slightly. In Nevada City, the most important mining town in California at the time, pioneer Luzena Wilson recalled that, "The feminine portion of the population was so small that I have had men come forty miles over the mountains just to look at me, and I never was called a handsome woman, in my best days, even by my most ardent admirers." Wilson was not even single at the time.

A Live Woman in the Mines, *1853, by Charles Nahl*

The number of unmarried men in California during the Gold Rush was widely perceived as a problem. There were reports of extreme debauchery and some felt these wild men needed taming: "Among the many privations and deteriorating influences to which the thousands who are flocking thither will be subjected, one of the greatest is the absence of women, with all her kindly cares and powers," commented the social reformer Eliza Farnham. In 1849, Farnham decided to take matters into her own hands, in part because following the death of her husband she was planning to move with her two young sons to San Francisco, where she had inherited property. She placed an ad looking for "intelligent, virtuous and efficient women" who were over the age of twenty-five and could contribute $250 to the price of passage from New York to the West Coast on the ship the *Angelique*. Local newspapers gushed approvingly: "Eliza Farnham and her girls are coming, and the dawning of brighter days for our golden land is even now perceptible. The day of regeneration is nigh at hand," according to the *Alta California*. In the end only three women agreed to sail with her, in part due to rumors that Farnham's real intention was to lure them into a life of vice.

California's fast-growing cities embraced personal ads with vigor. They first appeared in the *San Francisco Chronicle* in the 1860s, for example from "a young man of 27, of sober and steady habits" who explained that "Being a stranger in this city, would take this mode of making the acquaintance of some lady or widow with a view to matrimony." Herein was the contrary nature of matchmaking: it was tricky when there were too few options, but it was also tricky when there were too many. During the 1860s, the population of San Francisco increased threefold, to about 150,000, and it was not long before one or two personal ads were appearing in the *San Francisco Chronicle* every day.

The women who advertised in the *San Francisco Chronicle* were typically "a young widow lady in reduced circumstances," "a lady, well situated but a stranger in the city," or sometimes "a young lady, full of life and fun, 21 years of age, [who] would like to get acquainted with several gentlemen of means. Object—Matrimony." The latter recalls the sorts of ads that got the *New York Herald* into trouble around the same time, with the phrase "Object—Matrimony" used as an afterthought to get past the censors. Most were looking for the likes of "a gentleman of means and respectability, of good personal appearance and sensible age." There were not as many ads from women as in other states, however, because the labor shortage in the West opened up new opportunities for women to be financially independent: Nellie Pooler Chapman took over her husband's dental practice, for example, when he deserted her for the silver mines, and in 1879 she became the first registered woman dentist in California.

San Francisco Chronicle, *April 11, 1873*

Meanwhile, men who appeared in the personals of the *San Francisco Chronicle* included "a young Nevada merchant, aged 33, in satisfactory circumstances," "a young man lately from the East who has saved $2,000 from his labor," "a working man who is tired of living in restaurants," and a "young gentleman, 24 years of age, of high literary attainments" who lived in Green River, Wyoming. They most commonly wanted a wife who was "respectable," "industrious," or, ideally, both; this tough frontier society demanded nothing less. Some sought to manifest the most typically Victorian wife possible, for example, a "healthy, intelligent young woman of plain quiet habits and a cheerful but not too positive disposition." Others specifically sought out an East Coast girl: a thirty-five-year-old San Francisco businessman advertised in the *New York Herald* for "a warm-hearted and amiable young lady of about 25," stipulating that any replies needed to reach him speedily because he was heading back west on the steamship the following week and hoped to have a new wife to accompany him on the voyage.

Personal ads were also increasingly popular in Los Angeles and in Sacramento where, in 1883, in between a "Lost!" ad for a large brass key and a shout-out for a new "elegant first-class hotel," there was an ad that read simply: "I want to marry a young lady—blonde preferred. Must be a resident of this city."

Men living in California's mining communities found the personals a very useful resource. It was tough to persuade local women to join them due to a culture of violence, extreme isolation, and dangerous working conditions. Women slept in tents, sat on boxes, cooked over campfires, and gave birth alone. According to Louise Clappe, who came out from New Jersey with her husband, one winter in the camp at Plumas they ran out of food and had to survive solely on dried mackerel and "wagon loads of hard, dark hams . . . [that] nothing but the sharpest knife and stoutest heart can penetrate." Nonetheless, it suited some. "I like this wild and barbarous life," wrote Clappe, another time telling her sister Molly that "everybody ought to go to the mines, just to see how little it takes to make people comfortable in the world."

Woman at Auburn Ravine, *1852, attributed to photographer Joseph B. Starkweather*

Annie Gayle was one of the prettiest girls in Akron, Ohio. She worked as a seamstress, but was desperately bored and on the lookout for a chance to head west. When she spotted an ad from a man living in a mining community in French Camp, California, who was after an adventurous wife with whom to experience frontier life, she quickly decided that he was the one for her.

California held a particular appeal for girls like Annie. In 1849, the state's newly created constitution radically reformed property law with the specific intention of increasing female immigration to the state. Women were at last permitted to keep their own property once they married, rather than having it immediately transfer to their husband. The state's booming economy, along with its liberal divorce laws, made it an attractive destination for women who sought equality and freedom.

Some women were persuaded to risk the long, arduous journey by the fantasy of the West portrayed in trashy magazines and dime novels. Popular writers like Owen Wister created characters deep in the Western psyche of the tough, plucky frontier woman who could skin a buffalo while wrestling a Native American to the ground and barely break a sweat or have her headscarf out of place. There was a perception that the West Coast offered excitement and adventure—a welcome escape from the repressive social mores of life back east.

On September 10, 1894, aged just sixteen, Annie stepped off the train in Sacramento, California, fresh-faced and eager even after a journey west of more than 2,500 miles. The man meeting her was a handsome forty-something named Horace Knapp who, in letters, had described himself as "a good fellow, with means and prospects." From the station, they headed to dinner, where they agreed to be married the next day.

Horace and Annie settled into a small cabin in the San Juan Valley, where he invested all her savings into a mining venture. He was often away, but she assumed he was hard at work building their future together.

One night, a little boy dressed in rags brought Annie a note.

"Mrs. Knapp, your husband has another wife living not far from you," it read. "He has three children whom he has deserted. He married you to get whatever money you had."

Annie confronted Horace as soon as he got home, but he denied everything.

A few days later, she secretly followed him into a dilapidated building and up a flight of wooden stairs. A rickety door was opened by a tired-looking woman in a calico wrapper with three small children clinging to her legs.

"Who are you?" asked Annie.

"I am Mrs. Horace Knapp," the woman answered flatly.

On her mantelpiece was a photograph of Horace. He ended up being charged with bigamy and sent to prison.

Farmers found it no easier than miners to find a wife. In 1903, Byron Shaffer, a Ventura County farmer, mailed a photo of himself and his family to a woman named Margaret Adams, whom he had met through a personal ad.

Byron and his six children from his first wife

Margaret agreed to marry him, whether despite or because of his six children. The ceremony took place at her home in Pella, Marion County, Iowa, on October 12.

Wedding photo of Byron and Margaret

The newlyweds immediately returned west to Ventura County, where they settled into farming life and had five more children, including Lacy Elmer Shaffer. Lacy appears in the photograph on the next page (he is the figure on the far left with his bicycle) and was later the grandfather of George Mouchet, who was kind enough to write to me about this piece of hidden family history.

Byron and Margaret and their children

The Shaffers later moved to Santa Cruz, where Byron lived until his death in 1937, while Margaret sadly died in a mental institution in 1943.

Washington was the slowest of all the states to turn to personal ads, in part because newspapers remained rare in this remote frontier territory. But in 1893 a "middle aged man, with a good farm" in Mason County advertised for "a lady in the twenties with some money; Scandinavian preferred," and from then on this kind of approach became more widespread.

By the turn of the century, there was a marriage ad to suit almost everyone.

> Young man, moderate circumstances, and who has glass eye, would like to form the acquaintance of young girl who also has a glass eye or some other deformity not more severe; girl must be respectable; money unnecessary; object matrimony.

This ad appeared in the *New York Times* in 1903, but was reprinted in newspapers across the country. The railway inspector who placed the ad later explained to a journalist that, having lost an eye in an accident at work, "I think it wiser of me to marry a girl who has some personal defect so that she will not be so apt to fling up my deformity should we ever be so unfortunate as to quarrel." Sensible indeed. Note, too, the importance placed on compatibility. There really could be someone out there for everybody, if only you looked in the personals.

John

Minnesota, 1910

I wanted a family.

A wife, some children, then a long life together, growing old.

I also wanted to know what sex was like. Sex with a woman, that is.

But there were very few women around and I could barely speak English, although I was taking lessons with an eighty-year-old clergyman who lived just across the river.

I didn't bother telling my brothers about my plan. I wanted to surprise them by bringing home a ravishing wife in a blue dress with a wide smile.

I hoped for someone like me. Swedish or Norwegian would do. Industrious. Ambitious. Excited for a fresh start. It had been a tough couple of years: I had had an ongoing, terrible toothache, we had lost seven of our cows to disease, and, worst of all, the house I was halfway through building got swept away in a tornado. It was tough out here—tougher than I expected when I set sail from home. America looked different in the brochures.

Then one day when I was round at my neighbor's house, there was a "Husband Wanted" ad in his copy of the local newspaper. I'd never seen or heard of such a thing back in Sweden, but here everything was different, even love and marriage.

Why not, I thought to myself? What did I have to lose?

And so, I decided to answer an advertisement.

CHAPTER ELEVEN

"TRIFLERS NEED NOT APPLY": INDIANA, 1908

Just before dawn one foggy Monday, in the spring of 1908 in the small town of La Porte, Indiana, Joe Maxson, a tall, pale farmhand with an impressive mustache, woke to the smell of smoke.

Joe's bedroom was directly above the kitchen, so he figured his employer, Belle Gunness, must be getting a head start on breakfast. He rolled over and went back to sleep. He felt unusually groggy; he would later wonder whether this was the result of a slightly strange-tasting orange Belle had given him to eat the night before.

It was not long, however, before Joe realized that this was more than just everyday stove smoke. He leapt out of bed in his long underwear and ran to the window. Flames were darting out of the kitchen below. The whole house was on fire!

Frantically pulling on his clothes and boots, Joe raced to the connecting door to the main house. He tried to kick it down in order to warn Belle, her servant Jennie, and her three children, who were all asleep inside, but to no avail.

Choking from the thick smoke and barely able to see, Joe darted down the stone staircase and began to shout at the top of his voice.

Belle Gunness

"Wake up! Wake up, I tell you!"

He threw brick after brick at the window, but all he could hear was the continued roaring of the enormous flames.

Suddenly, a beam gave way, sending furniture from the upper floors tumbling down in a cascade of sparks.

Within minutes, a couple of neighbors from nearby farms galloped up on their horses to see if they could help. Someone had the idea to send for the local sheriff. Al Smutzer was a rotund, red-faced, curly-haired man who wore a dark-colored turtleneck and a leather peaked cap. His red Ford truck was soon heading up to the farm.

Despairingly, the assembled group watched as the entire property was reduced to heaps of charred, smoking debris. When daylight broke, Smutzer ordered teams of men from La Porte's volunteer fire service to search for the bodies of those believed to be in the house.

For hours, they found nothing.

But a little before five in the afternoon, while excavating the cellar, someone's shovel uncovered a human hand. More digging found four bodies, huddled together like they were sheltering from a storm: a woman, two girls, and a boy.

The woman was headless though, which was odd.

A few days later, Asle Helgelien arrived at the Gunness farm in search of his brother, Andrew, who had gone missing, the only clues to his whereabouts a few letters from Belle. Asle was immediately suspicious. He asked Joe if he knew of any holes that had been dug in the garden in recent months, which he did. The two of them grabbed a couple of shovels and got to work. The stench was appalling: Joe was sure it was old fish cans, until they got to about four feet down and hit upon something hard covered with a hessian sack. It was a human neck and arm. More digging revealed the arms, legs, and head, all of which had been neatly cut away from the torso.

Sheriff Smutzer organized a search of the rest of the property. By the next day, five more bodies had been found. Then more the next day, and the next. Within a week of the fire, the tally was up to thirty-five. Most had been brutally dismembered, wrapped in a piece of burlap, and buried in the chicken yard or the pig pen.

Belle Gunness was revealed to be the most prolific female serial killer of all time.

Over forty reporters descended on La Porte, along with thousands of gawkers. The murders were front-page news across the country. The families of missing men from across the Midwest soon arrived, too, hoping that at last they might discover the fate of their loved ones.

But one aspect of the case mystified everyone. How had Belle Gunness managed to lure so many men to her farm? Rude comments were made about her physical appearance and demeanor, while many speculated about the sexual services she must have offered.

The answer was simple. Belle had exploited one of the many innovations that, in 1908, were well on the way to helping transform America from a Victorian society to a modern one: marriage ads.

Belle Gunness was born Brynhild Storset on the west coast of Norway in 1859. She was the youngest of eight children of Paul Storset, a stonemason, and his wife, Berit, and grew up in a fishing and farming hamlet in an agricultural region best known for its elaborate knitting patterns.

As a child, Belle was shy and unassuming. Her teacher at the Evangelical Lutheran Church, where she was confirmed in 1874, remembered her as an exemplary student, although years later, with the benefit of hindsight, neighbors told the local newspaper that she was "a very bad human being, capricious and extremely malicious."

Belle's nickname at school was "Snurkvistpala," a combination of the Norwegian words *snurkvist* (spruce twigs) and *pala* (Paul's daughter). This was a not-so-subtle attempt by her classmates to humiliate her: her family was so poor that she was indeed forced to collect her own spruce twigs from the mountain slopes every day after school to use as kindling.

At fourteen, Belle started working as a cattle girl for surrounding farms, taking her employers' herds to nearby pastures to forage for food. She was remembered as a hard worker, but it was a dull, difficult existence. She had to get up early to milk the cows, spend the day with them up the mountain, bed them down at night, and then churn all the cream into butter before collecting her wages.

Perhaps Belle dealt with the drudgery by telling stories with the other cattle girls. Norway has a fierce tradition of folklore and they had all grown up with the *huldre* women, fairy creatures whose cows' tails revealed their inhuman nature to their mortal husbands, and the *gjoyer*, female trolls who lumbered through the mountains. Belle herself was to grow into a woman whose malevolence seemed to match that of the unseen creatures peopling Norwegian folk tradition.

According to local gossip, in 1877, at the age of eighteen, Belle got pregnant. This would have been scandal enough to ruin her, but worse was to come.

Belle was propositioned at a local country dance by the son of a wealthy landowner. When she resisted, he kicked her in the stomach and she miscarried. He was never prosecuted, but he soon fell ill and died from a mysterious stomach ailment. There were whispers that Belle had poisoned him, but no one could prove it. It is possible, though, that this traumatic event contributed to the violent attitude she developed toward men.

It was not long afterward that Belle's older sister, Nellie, sailed for the New World.

The first fifty-two Norwegian emigrants to head to America arrived in 1825 on board a sloop-style ship called the *Restauration*. Most were Quakers from rural areas in search of religious freedom following years of repression by the Lutheran state church. Many more followed in the ensuing decades in search of economic opportunity, a tide that crested after the devastating famine of 1866–1868, when over 110,000 made the journey. Most settled briefly in New York before heading further west to Illinois or perhaps Wisconsin or Minnesota.

Some found encouragement in 19th-century Norwegian literature, which portrayed the New World as a fairy tale made real. In Ole Rolvaag's classic novel *Giants in the Earth*, the protagonist renames himself Ash Boy, the hero of many Norwegian folktales, when he settles on the Dakota plains. Publicity brochures published by railroad companies and letters home from Norwegian immigrants confirmed the connection, describing America as a land of opportunity where the rag-to-riches myth really did come true.

Belle hated being left behind. She quickly found herself a job on a bigger farm where the wages were higher and every day for three years she milked the cows, fed the horses, and cleaned out the hog pen, falling exhaustedly into bed at night.

It took Belle until 1881 to save enough money to buy herself a passage to New York. She became part of a second, even larger wave of mass emigration from Norway—a response to Norway's industrial slowdown. Within a decade, a ninth of the country's population had left.

She set sail aboard the steamship the SS *Tasso* of the Wilson Line: it departed from Trondheim in Norway, there was a stop-off in Hull in England, and then came the eight-week Atlantic crossing. The diarist Ingeborg Olsdatter Øye wrote a vivid account of a journey on board the same ship the year before:

> There are about 400 emigrants aboard the ship. It is a terrible mess since most of them are seasick . . . The worst is the bad sleeping accommodations we have, so full and crowded as it is too . . . We are now out on the North Sea, so we cannot see land in any direction . . . I got up to get a little something to eat, namely a slice of bread and some biscuits which we receive in the morning with a cup of bad black coffee . . . Today it is quite busy up on deck, some are washing themselves, others are writing . . . The wind is blowing cold and strong, and the seas washes over the deck at times.

Belle, however, could not care less about the hardship. She was too happy to be out of Norway and too excited for what the future held; as Theodore Dreiser put it in *Sister Carrie*, she was "life-hungry."

When twenty-two-year-old Belle reached the front of the line at Castle Garden (the same one Augusta Larsen would stand in two years later), the immigration officer struggled with her first name, Brynhild. Too weary to argue, she agreed to change it to Belle. She was more than ready to adopt a new identity, and this was the perfect opportunity to do so. Her occupation was listed as "domestic servant."

Once she received her papers, she headed to the station for a train to Chicago.

When Belle stepped down onto the platform in Chicago, her first impressions were probably similar to those of the novelist Hamlin Garland: "I shall never forget the feeling of dismay with which . . . I perceived from the car window a huge smoke-cloud which embraced the eastern horizon, for this, I was told, was the soaring banner of the great and gloomy inland metropolis . . ." Garland went on to sketch a frightening portrait of the hackmen who grabbed his baggage then charged him an outrageous fare to drive him to his hotel. Their eyes were "cynical," their hands "clutching, insolent, terrifying," their faces "remorseless, inhuman and mocking," their grins like "those of wolves." The implication was that the city had a way of turning its residents to the dark side.

Belle headed straight to the house her sister Nellie shared with her new husband, John Larsen, on the northwest side of the city. She initially took a job as a domestic servant, cooking and babysitting for rich families. Later, she found employment at a butcher's shop where she learned to slice up animal carcasses; she was a tall, strong, muscular woman and well suited to the work. But the job was never going to lead to the easy life she had dreamed of as a teenager herding cattle. She needed a new plan.

Belle's relationship with her sister became increasingly strained, so Nellie was delighted when, in 1884, Belle met and married a department store security guard named Mads Sorenson. Together they opened a confectionary store in the Austin area of the city, living upstairs and settling into a busy life among Chicago's huge Scandinavian population.

The store flourished, in large part because her husband Mads was so popular with customers. Belle, however, told her sister that, "I would never remain with this man if it wasn't for the nice home he had . . ." The couple started to quarrel about money; she suggested he increase his life insurance coverage, which he obediently did. A neighbor later commented that, "She seldom spoke, even when addressed, and her husband it appeared would almost crouch at her approach. He looked to be in fear of her."

There was gossip about the babies who lived at 58 Marian Court. Neighbors were confused about where they came from, as Belle never looked pregnant. There was lurid talk that the confectionary store was a front for a baby farm that bought and sold newborns.

One of the children, Caroline, died aged just three months of inflammation of the large intestine, a condition that can result from poisoning. Another named Axel died of the same in 1898. In both instances, Belle collected large insurance checks.

On July 30, 1900, Mads died of unknown causes on the only day on which two life insurance policies on him overlapped. An inquest was ordered, but never carried out.

In 1901, Belle used the insurance money she had collected to purchase a farm in the small town of La Porte, Indiana. She took to raising pigs, and neighbors noted that she slaughtered them herself with great mastery. This mirrored the way the American workforce was transitioning under the influence of industrialization: traditional gender roles were beginning to blur.

Wild rumors spread among the townsfolk that Belle was a man in disguise. The local coroner would later describe her as "a woman of unusual appearance. She was large, bony, powerful looking, with square jaws and black eyes." He went on to comment on "her lack of womanly appearance." A neighbor remembered her "large, grotesque" hands, while another described the wide leather holster belt filled with knives she always wore.

On April Fool's Day, 1902, Belle married Peter Gunness, a Norwegian hog farmer whom she had first met when he lodged with her in Chicago during the World's Fair of 1893.

Just a week after the ceremony, Peter's infant daughter died of uncertain causes while alone in the house with Belle.

Not long afterward, a baby named Phillip Gunness appeared. Belle forbade anyone to help with the birth, then just two days later she was spotted out in the yard chasing after her pigs. When the midwife Mary Swenson arrived, she discovered that the baby was already washed and clothed and looked too old to be a newborn. The suspicion was that Belle had faked the pregnancy, then passed the baby, likely a foundling, off as her own.

A few months later, Peter Gunness was found dead with his skull smashed in. At the inquest, Belle claimed his death was a terrible accident: according to her, he had been sitting by the kitchen stove when a sausage grinder fell off a shelf onto his head. Belle testified that Peter "was a very nice man. I wouldn't have married him if I had not thought him nice . . . I never heard him say a word out of the way so long as he was here." When asked whether she had ever been afraid that somebody might have hit him with the sausage grinder, she replied, "I have never been afraid at all."

Peter's death netted Belle $3,000 in insurance money. Locals refused to believe that her husband could be so clumsy; he had run a hog farm on the property and was known to be an experienced butcher. The district coroner reviewed the case and announced that Peter had been murdered. He convened a coroner's jury to look into the matter, but it went no further.

Poisoning is a very impersonal form of murder, but bashing your husband's head in with a sausage grinder really steps up the level of violence. When Belle managed to get away with it, she must have felt invulnerable. The only conundrum now was how and where to find her next victim, or victims.

In 1905, Belle began to place marriage ads in a number of Chicago newspapers. Did one of the thousands of newspaper articles about Johann Hoch in 1905 inspire her to use the personals to find her victims? It seems likely. The personals offered a direct connection to those who were new in town, had few friends and no family, and were on the lookout for an opportunity—in other words, easy pickings.

> Comely widow who owns a large farm in one of the finest districts in La Porte County, Indiana, desires to make the acquaintance of a gentleman equally well provided, with view of joining fortunes. No replies by letter considered unless sender is willing to follow answer with personal visit. Triflers need not apply.

Belle had the most success with the *Skandinaven*, the first and best-selling of the numerous Norwegian-language newspapers recently established to meet the needs of the enormous Norwegian immigrant community: in 1900, a little over 40,000 Norwegians lived in Chicago, making it the third largest Norwegian city in the world after Oslo and Bergen. The *Skandinaven* was sold by newsboys at the train and bus stations and was frequently a newly arrived immigrant's first glimpse of the workings of the city.

In 1905, Belle claimed one of the first victims she found through a marriage ad, a farmhand named Henry Gurholt, who traveled from Iola, Wisconsin, in the hope of finding love.

Newspapers throughout Wisconsin such as the *Oshkosh Daily Northwestern* and the *Daily Milwaukee News* had carried marriage ads for years, mostly from men seeking women, for example from a "gentleman of refinement, nice looking and stylish, with correct morals" who sought a mate who was musically inclined; "A German, aged thirty, owner of property" who sought a "young Catholic"; and "A farmer [who] wishes to correspond with a farmer's widow or daughter." A woman seeking a man was something of a novelty.

Upon arriving in La Porte, Gurholt wrote home that "he is in good health, and that he likes the farm where he is—that on the farm there are apple trees, pear trees, and peach trees, and that they are starting to blossom" then went on to ask for "ten or fifteen bushels of seed potatoes to be mailed to him," according to a later deposition given by his brother Martin.

Gurholt's family never heard from him again. They wrote to Belle to ask his whereabouts, and her reply "was a very sympathizing letter, expressing regret that we had lost sight of my brother. She said he had left her place and gone with some horse traders to Chicago, but that if she should ever hear of him, she would let us know immediately."

Gurholt's trunk, however, remained at Belle's house, as did his favorite fur overcoat, which she took to wearing around the farm whenever the wind got chilly.

Not long afterward, Belle lured another Norwegian immigrant, George Anderson from Tarkio, Missouri, to live with her. One night, while sleeping in the guest room, Anderson woke with a start to see Belle standing over him, holding a candle in her hand and peering into his eyes. He later stated that the expression on her face was so sinister and murderous that he let out a loud yell and she immediately ran from the room without uttering a word. Anderson jumped out of bed, threw on his clothes, and fled the house without saying goodbye. He boarded the first train back to Missouri and never returned for his belongings.

Anderson was the only one of Belle's suitors to leave the Gunness farm alive.

In 1906, John Moe from Elbow Lake, a small agricultural town in Minnesota, responded to a marriage ad in the *Skandinaven*. Ads from women seeking men had been appearing in local newspapers like the *Minneapolis Journal* and the *St. Paul Globe* since the 1870s; they included a "Lady of 50 . . . poor but good," a "Blue-eyed blond lady of nineteen, sweet, refined nature," and, as always, lots of widows. The one Moe answered did not appear much different.

The pair exchanged letters for months, with Belle repeatedly asking him to come and share both her bed and her farm. Moe was last seen in his hometown on December 20, 1906; two days later, a cashier remembered him coming in to the bank in La Porte, "very anxious" to withdraw a large amount of cash.

Moe was never seen again.

A carpenter who sometimes worked for Belle, Emil Greening, later told investigators that he thought it was strange at the time that Moe's trunk had not disappeared with him: "His was not the only one. There were about fifteen other trunks, and one room was packed full of all kinds of men's clothing which Mrs. Gunness said her 'cousins' had left and she was not certain if they would be back for them." Yet still no one suspected the truth.

Around this time, a coachman dropped a servant girl named Addie Landis off at the Gunness farm. She ran up to the back door and peered through the window to see if anyone was home. Letting out a bloodcurdling scream, she came stumbling back, telling the coachman, "I've seen the most awful thing I ever expect to see!" and raving incoherently about someone cutting up a body. He took her back to the train station, but within a week Addie had a breakdown and was committed to the Logansport State Hospital for the Insane for the rest of her life.

In 1907, Andrew Helgelien galloped up to Belle's farm. He was apprehensive but excited. Andrew was forty-nine years old and an immigrant from Sweden, but had built a life for himself as a farmer in Aberdeen, South Dakota; now all he needed was a wife.

Women were scarce in South Dakota. A local newspaper ran a series of reports about the "genuine girl famine" in the state: "two or three carloads could be readily distributed in towns like Huron, Aberdeen, Watertown, Sioux Falls, and Mitchell." As a local hotelier commented, "husbands in South Dakota are as abundant as blackberries in July." Turning to the personals for help must have seemed like a sensible move.

Helgelien corresponded with Belle for over two years. The letters make for fascinating reading. "You impress me with being a good man with a strong and honest character," Belle wrote alluringly. "A real genuine Norwegian in every respect and it is difficult to find such a man and not every woman appreciates. There are plenty of those Americans or 'doll men' [gigolos] around here but I would not even look at them. Take all of your money out of the bank as soon as possible then get ready as soon as you can . . ." She tried to persuade him to visit with promises of "good homemade cake and some good coffee and cream pudding" and a pencil drawing of the two of them snuggled up together by the fire.

Helgelien eventually succumbed to Belle's epistolary charms. He caught a train to Minneapolis, connected to Chicago, and rode on horseback into the Indiana countryside. When he at last reached Belle's isolated farm, he tied his horse up to a gatepost, took the steps up to the front door two at a time, and knocked eagerly. Belle opened the door—she was not quite as attractive as the way she had described herself in her letters, but no matter—and ushered Helgelien in. The door banged behind him.

Helgelien was Belle's final victim before the fire, which uncovered all sorts of secrets.

Investigators managed to piece together exactly how Belle Gunness killed her victims. She poisoned them by adding strychnine to their dinner, then dragged them down to the farmhouse's basement where she would lay them on a large wooden table and use her skills as a butcher to dismember them. She would then throw the torso into a vat filled with chloride of lime solution and wrap the remaining body parts in sackcloth and bury them all over the farm, pouring quicklime over them to speed up decomposition. She fed the leftovers to the pigs. Belle is thought to have done this to about forty men.

In November 1908, one of Belle's farmhands, Ray Lamphere, was put on trial for arson. Lamphere had had an on-off sexual relationship with Belle, but she later accused him of stalking her. When a local youth swore to police that he saw the farmhand running away from the house shortly after the first flames shot from the roof, police went to Lamphere's house to arrest him; when they arrived, he was waiting on the stairs, wearing an overcoat that belonged to the murdered John Moe and a watch that belonged to the murdered Henry Gurhold.

The case turned into a bitter public battle between local Republicans and Democrats. The Republican sheriff Smutzer was about to retire and his deputy, William Anstiss, wanted his job. It was in both their interests to bring the culprits to justice and move on. Democrats, however, saw this as an opportunity to discredit their opponents. The two local papers, the (Republican) *Daily Herald* and the (Democrat) *Argus Bulletin*, also divided along party lines.

A huge number of witnesses were called and all sorts of salacious details were revealed. At one point the prosecuting lawyer asked a friend of Lamphere's, "Did he tell you that he slept with Mrs. Gunness?"

"No."

"He didn't say he slept with her?"

"No. He said she slept with him."

The courtroom exploded into laughter and the judge had to bang his gavel repeatedly to restore order.

The farmhand Joe Moxson later testified about the night before the fire. The whole household had supper together at about 6.30 P.M.: "Bread and butter, dried beef, salmon, beefsteak and potatoes. After supper, we played games. The main one was 'Little Red Riding Hood and the Fox.' Mrs. Gunness loved to play this game, and almost cried if the bad fox chanced to catch Red Riding Hood. At 8.30 P.M. I became sleepy and went upstairs to bed in my room above the kitchen. The last I saw of Mrs. Gunness, she was sitting on the floor with the children, playing with the toy engines and passenger coaches."

On the night before Thanksgiving, Lamphere was found guilty of arson. When the judge asked him if he had any reasons why sentencing should not be pronounced on him, he mysteriously replied, "I have none—now." He died in jail a few weeks later.

There was still a major piece of the puzzle missing, though.

Belle's head.

If it really was her body that investigators found in the cellar, where was her head?

Add to this the testimony by the doctor who carried out the postmortem that the body brought to the morgue was both five inches shorter and fifty pounds lighter than Belle. The hands were manicured, which Belle's never were. Furthermore, Belle's dentist testified that she had a number of gold fillings in her teeth, which would have been impossible to destroy in the fire. So why were they not found in the rubble, despite an extensive search?

Gradually, the whispers started. Belle was not dead after all. She had murdered her children (if they even were her real children), plus another unfortunate woman to throw people off the trail, set fire to her house, and escaped to Chicago, or New York, or California.

Sheriff Smutzer later commented, that "There were forty-five correspondents in La Porte at the time of the case and not one of them believed that Mrs. Gunness escaped." He claimed that a reporter from the *Chicago American* came up with the sensational story of Belle's survival as a ploy to sell more newspapers.

But this still did not explain what happened to Belle's head.

Her photograph was sent to police agencies across the country. Over the years, there were multiple supposed sightings. In 1931, a woman named Esther Carlson was arrested in Los Angeles for poisoning a man with arsenic and many who saw her picture in the paper noticed her strong resemblance to Belle Gunness. She died before further investigations could be made; a DNA test in 2007 proved inconclusive. What really happened to Belle Gunness, or even how many people she killed, remains a mystery.

Lucy

New York City, 1968

The doctor prescribed me my Pill—with a lecherous wink and a rub of my arm, but perhaps that was just the price to be paid?

I did want a husband, but it seemed dull to snap one up right away.

I liked all the frantic parties.

I liked my job at the insurance company.

I liked drinking a Mai Tai or three with my girlfriends on a Friday night.

I was shy, though. And not the prettiest. I also had a strong preference for larger men.

Why the hell not?

And so, I decided to answer an advertisement.

CHAPTER TWELVE

LOOKING FOR LOVE IN MODERN AMERICA: C. 1908–2020

B elle swiped left. Not Scandinavian enough. She swiped again. Too muscly. And again. Too close to his family. The next face that appeared on her screen, however, had potential: a recent immigrant, slight build, eager face. Just what she was looking for.

Imagine for a moment that Belle Gunness had used Tinder. One shudders at how many victims she could have lured to her home via social media; what an enormous body count it would have been.

Gunness and Tinder feel like entities from different planets, and yet they existed just a hundred years apart—a hundred years, however, when almost everything changed with regard to how humans choose a mate.

The year 1908, when Sheriff Smutzer made his grisly discovery at Gunness's farmhouse, represented a moment in the early 20th century when America began to lose its innocence. The nation was living through a period of enormous progress under Teddy Roosevelt: the first around-the-world car race began in New York and the first sorority for black college-educated women was established—also signaling that higher education, specifically colleges and universities once prohibited for black Americans, was now an integral aspect of society. Yet with progress came problems, and the widespread newspaper coverage of Gunness was in part a response to the way the case served to confirm a number of preexisting contemporary anxieties about the impact of modernization on the nation's moral compass.

The popularity of personal ads plummeted drastically in the years immediately afterward. They became mostly the preserve of niche romantic desires, such as the 1911 ad from "A collector of postage stamps, possessing 12,544 specimens [who] desires to contract a marriage with a young lady, also a collector, who has the blue Mauritius stamp of 1847" or the ad in the *Washington Post* four months after America entered World War II from a "Successful business man" looking for an "extra large, extremely stout lady between 30 and 40; object, matrimony; only one who will appreciate unusual comforts and will give full description in first letter need reply."

Personal ads also remained a lifeline for those in more isolated areas. I recently received an email from Linda Vixie about her great-grandfather, William Wepsala. William emigrated from Finland in the early 1890s to become a homesteader just south of Fort Morgan, Colorado, later moving to Denver where he worked as a roofer. On January 17, 1915, he placed an ad in the *Denver Post* following the death of his first wife from appendicitis:

Denver Post, *January 17, 1915*

Despite the offensive tone of his ad—"living man's widow and colored women keep hands off"—less than two months later William married Nellie Blattenburg, a fifty-seven-year-old widow from Iowa now living in Trinidad, Colorado.

The marriage did not last long, in part because William repeatedly borrowed money from Nellie (her first husband was a successful dairy farmer, so she had cash to spare) and on October 21, 1916, they legally separated.

William Wepsala (1861–1944)

Nellie Blattenburg (1857–1920)

Nellie died in 1920. William spent some time in California, then returned to Colorado to live with his daughter from his first marriage; family lore had it that he always used to put a candle in a coffee can and take it up to bed with him, terrifying everyone that he would burn the house down. He later suffered from dementia and died in the Colorado State Hospital in 1944.

Despite the many successful (and unsuccessful) marriages orchestrated via a newspaper, the public reputation of advertising for love continued to falter from the 1930s to the 1950s. In those years, personal ads were carried only by the *Saturday Review* and a few pornographic magazines.

What replaced personal ads during this period? In the years after World War I, courtship changed drastically. The level of parental supervision decreased: in the 1922 edition of Emily Post's famous book on etiquette there was a chapter about "The Chaperone and Other Conventions," but by 1927 it had been retitled "The Vanishing Chaperone and Other New Conventions," and by 1937 "The Vanished Chaperone and Other Lost Conventions." One result was that "None of the Victorian mothers . . . had any idea how casually their daughters were accustomed to be kissed," according to F. Scott Fitzgerald.

The concept of the "date" gained in popularity, in part because it took place outside the home. Dance halls and movie theaters offered the perfect public spaces, while "petting parties" were a regular feature of high school life in the 1920s. The number of students attending college tripled between 1890 and 1920, and by 1927 the majority of colleges were coed and students were able to mix freely, making this a great place to meet your future husband or wife. And, crucially, the number of cars on America's roads tripled between 1919 and 1929. As the sociologist Robert Cooley Angell noted in 1928, "The ease with which a couple can secure absolute privacy when in possession of a car and the spirit of reckless abandon which high speed and moonlight drives engender have combined to break down the traditional barriers." There were far more ways to meet a mate than ever before, and hence less need to turn to the newspapers.

But the reputational damage inflicted on personal ads by newspaper stories about the ads' dark consequences had the most impact of all. Examples include Helmuth Schmidt of Michigan, who was arrested in 1918 for murdering over thirty women he met through ads in German-language newspapers, as well as other "Lonely Hearts Killers" like Eva Brandon Rablen in 1929, Nannie Doss in

1927–1954, Harry Powers in 1927–1931, and Raymond Fernandez and Martha Beck in 1947–1949. These are just the well-known ones. The *New York Times* regularly featured terrible accounts of someone (usually a woman) killed by a partner met through the personals. A sample headline in 1921 read, "Marriage 'Ad' Wife Is Found Slain." Isabella Dobson was beaten and choked to death in her bungalow in Camden, just south of Philadelphia; her husband, George Dobson, whom she had met through an ad, was the prime suspect.

Whether there actually were more "Lonely Hearts Killers" than there had been fifty years earlier is debatable. It is more likely that just more of them got caught, in part due to improved police techniques, in particular advances in forensic science. In 1892, British scientist Francis Galton published evidence that the chance of two individuals having identical fingerprints was 1 in 64 billion, thereby providing the scientific basis for them to be used in court for the first time; eight years later, Austrian doctor Karl Landsteiner discovered the existence of variations in human blood types, which would transform the way detectives could analyze the blood found at a crime scene. At the same time, increased community ties, particularly among first-generation immigrants, meant people no longer disappeared quite so easily into the chaos of the city or the quiet of the frontier without anyone noticing. Nonetheless, salacious newspaper coverage skewed public perception for several decades.

Then came the Sexual Revolution, and no one really cared about perception any more. In 1960, G.D. Searle & Company, based in Illinois, submitted a new product named Enovid to the Food and Drug Administration for approval. It was the world's first contraceptive pill and it proved an instant hit: within five years, 6.5 million American women were taking it, encouraging the uncoupling of marriage and sex once and for all. The zeitgeist of freedom, individualism, and rebellion against social mores led to something of a comeback for personal ads.

New York's *Village Voice* began running personals in the early 1960s. They were hugely popular from the beginning and provided both content and income for this fledgling, scrappy newspaper. According to its publisher, John B. Evans:

> Anytime I was at a party, the conversation would immediately turn
> to personals. Everybody wanted to know about them. Usually they
> would turn up their noses and mutter a few words of sympathy for

the poor, pathetic human beings who had to resort to advertising. By the end of the evening, they were whispering in my ear, "So, John, tell me, do they *work*?"

Voice ads tended to be placed by upscale professionals like doctors, lawyers, and dentists, as well as a few from creatives like artists and musicians. Most were legit, but the language of some of them was unarguably risqué and contributed to the publication's reputation for scandal. A fifty-something architect named Mike Dreskey answered an ad from a woman calling herself a German governess:

> I figured she had been brought over from Europe to take care of somebody's kids, and she wanted to make friends. A few days later, I get this telephone call from a woman with a thick German accent, who says, "So you've been a naughty man?" She went on to tell me that certain men, particularly executives, needed to be whipped, beaten and humiliated. I thanked her for the information and hung up.

Or so he claimed.

In 1962, Illinois became the first state to legalize homosexuality, with others following suit not long afterward. Soon the first openly gay personal ads appeared, mostly in countercultural, fly-by-night pamphlets like *Trans-World Classifieds* or *Communique*. Among the first exclusively gay forums for personal ads was *Romans*, a Los Angeles–based publication launched in 1964. It pioneered some of the genre's earliest abbreviations like "A.L.A." (all letters answered); in every other way, however, the genre was not yet well-established enough to boast a jargon of its own, and so the simplicity of the language usually employed— "Man seeks man"—recalls some of the earliest heterosexual ads.

The heterosexual community soon incorporated its new sexual freedoms into personal ads. The first swingers' newspaper, *La Plume*, launched in 1955, featured ads from the start: "My husband and I wish to meet other attractive couples for broadminded friendship . . ." Some were probably fabricated by the editor to attract readers, but increasingly they were for real. In 1961, ads started to appear in the *San Francisco Chronicle* from "broad-minded couples." Dedicated magazines like *Swinger's Life* or *Kindred Spirits* carried plenty, too, and 1968 saw the first issue of the pornographic magazine *Screw*, which became well-known for its sex ads.

That same year, the *New York Review of Books* launched its personals column. The first ad appeared in its July 11 edition. "Wife wanted," it read. "Intelligent, beautiful, 18 to 25, broad-minded, sensitive, affectionate. For accomplished artist and exciting life." The use of the term "broad-minded" is interesting, but, as the magazine's business manager later commented, "It was the age of social exhibitionism. Everybody was letting it all hang out in other ways, so suddenly it was okay to display oneself in print." He went on, "In those days, it was very important to be 'self-aware.' So, you'd get ads like: 'Astrologer, 27, psychology student, desires to establish non-superficial friend-ship with sensitive, choicelessly aware persons who are non-self-oriented, deep, and wish to unearth real, person-ness relationships.'"

Compare the above to the ad placed in a New York newspaper one hundred and eighty years prior by "A young Gentleman of family and fortune" searching for a woman who was "under 40, not deformed, and in possession of at least one thousand pounds." Whereas advertisers used to conceal their individualisms, now they sought to celebrate it.

Until the end of the 1970s, ads in publications like the *New York Review of Books* tended to avoid words like "marriage" or "commitment." In 1975, *Singles News* launched in New York; its editor believed he was the first to dedicate a newspaper to personals, unaware of the likes of the *Matrimonial Times* and the *Marriage Gazette* a century earlier. Other mainstream publications followed: a 1979 ad in the *San Francisco Chronicle* from a "W/M 32 [who] seeks uninhibited female, 21–35, for dinner, movies and hot-tubs" was typical. Soon, there were magazines with ads aimed at all persuasions: *Sweet 'n' Sexy Seniors*, *Chocolate Singles*, the *Mensa Bulletin*. The largest personals magazine, *Intro*, was based in California and ran about a thousand ads a month. From the early 1980s, the phrase "I'm clean" started to crop up in response to the increasing risks of casual sex during the AIDS epidemic, recalling the way that "temperate habits" or "perfectly sober" featured in ads in the 1850s when the nation faced a different kind of public health crisis.

By the early 1980s, people in the *New York Review of Books* and beyond were once again looking for marriage. The publisher of the *Village Voice* estimated that

80 percent of advertisers wanted a permanent relationship; in gay magazines like the *New York Native*, it was about 50 percent. "Non-smoking" became a common demand in a prospective partner. The well-known abbreviation GSOH (good sense of humor) emerged in the late 1980s, as did WLTM (would like to meet), contributing to a developing collective lexicon. Other euphemisms included "Rubenesque" (plus-size), "living simply" (poor), and "sensuous" (interested in sex, not relationships). "Home-owning" was also used sometimes, but most tended to have a robust attitude to the economics of marriage, for example in the *San Francisco Chronicle* in 1985: "Attractive & successful young businessman, 32, would like to meet only a beautiful & classy lady 18–39 who is tired of working hard & wants to live well, laugh & love a lot. I'm only interested in a permanent living together relationship/ marriage without children. Prefer someone with experience. Or interest in Real Estate to help me with my business." This recalls ads like the one in the *New York Herald* a hundred years earlier from a gentleman looking for "a lady with some capital to form a business and matrimonial partnership. Being interested in a lucrative old established business, he wants to buy it out. Rare chance to acquire happiness and fortune honestly." Clearly, resources have always been a draw for both men and women.

In 1982, *New York* magazine began to feature personal ads. Within a couple of years, it averaged eighty-five a week and was deemed worthy of a long article in its own pages entitled "Romance in the Want Ads." The gist of it was that, for the first time, ads were fashionable. "Once considered the exclusive domain of social misfits and sexual deviants," the piece began, "the personals are rapidly becoming a respectable method of making social connections . . . Since personal ads are just now moving into the mainstream, there is still a lot of concern about the potential stigma." The classified-advertising manager of the *New York Review of Books* told the magazine that "A lot of people include apologies in their ads. They'll write, 'I'm not the type who usually places personal ads, and I hope you're not the type who usually answers them.'" It was a sentiment commonly expressed since the very earliest days of ads, albeit using different language.

Mel Worby, who was in charge of the personals for *New York* magazine at the time, revealed that "There is a lot of hand-holding in this job . . ." A journalist watched as he answered the phone, listened for a moment, sighed, and said, "Now, are you sure that you want to call yourself a 'luscious, leggy, single mom'?" He estimated that women received an average of forty replies, men fifteen. Among the successful ones was a thirty-year-old salesman named Les Degen, who in 1983 was encouraged by his roommate to place an ad in the magazine. One of the replies came from Long Island elementary-school teacher Gail Stein, whom he ended up marrying.

Les Degen and Gail Stein, who met through a personal ad in New York *magazine in 1984*

An ad in *New York* magazine did not always have the desired result, though. As one twenty-eight-year-old sobbed when interviewed in her Park Avenue apartment, "I went on 250 dates. I've never seen so many pink polyester sport coats in my life."

By the 1990s, approximately four out of five American newspapers carried personal ads. Advertisers were increasingly creative in their compositions, for example in the *San Francisco Chronicle* in 1998:

Snow White is frustrated. SWPF [Single White Professional Female], 41, tired of meeting Sneezy, Dopey, Grumpy, Sleepy, Crazy, Sleazy. Seeks smart, funny, romantic, attractive, dynamic, genuine, successful Prince Charming SWPM [Single White Professional Male], 38–48, NS [Non Smoking], who truly wants to be in a relationship and is ready for love, laughter and commitment with one terrific woman. White horse not necessary.

In 2001, the nation's paper of record proudly printed the following on its front page: "The New York Times Company announced yesterday that for the first time in its history, it would print personal advertising." It was not true that it was "the first time in its history," but apparently even the newspaper's own employees were unaware of the "man with glass eye seeking woman with glass eye" (and many thousands like him) who had graced its pages a century earlier.

Meanwhile, over the last fifty years, an entirely new medium for advertising for love had emerged: the Internet. It initially required a conceptual leap to allow matchmaking websites, and by extension science, to intervene in our romantic lives. But once this happened, many saw the benefits of removing some of the emotion from the matchmaking process and instead trusting in data. In some ways it represented the triumph of rationality over one of the least rational elements of the human existence: falling in love. Thus, computers revolutionized the matchmaking industry, forever changing our understanding of human mate choice. For some, it was a relief; for others, it was a disaster.

The earliest computers were essentially glorified calculators that emerged out of the business community. These mainframes were used within heavy industry and the U.S. military and space program. Computing capability advanced rapidly and in 1954, the world's first mass-produced computer, the IBM 650, was installed in the controller's department of the John Hancock Mutual Life Insurance Company in Boston. Early computers were extremely expensive and took up an entire room, which meant that the first experiments in computer dating occurred primarily on university campuses.

In 1959, two engineering students at Stanford, Phil Fialer and Jim Harvey, created the Happy Families Planning Services on the IBM 650 for a class project. They asked the 49 men and 49 women in their class to complete a questionnaire about their personality, religion, hobbies, height, and weight, then matched them up according to their answers. They succeeded, up to a point, receiving an A for the project and instigating one real-life marriage, but never took it any further.

The Happy Families Planning Services is generally considered the first experiment with computer dating, but Fialer and Harvey do not necessarily deserve all the glory; a number of similar projects were happening around the same time. Iowa State University initiated a project to match up a thousand students with a lengthy questionnaire which was then transferred onto punch cards and submitted to a computer. A few couples got together and *Life* magazine expressed an interest in publishing an article about it for its November edition, but then President John F. Kennedy was assassinated and no more was heard from them. Elsewhere, anyone's dad who was a computer engineer had access to a mainframe and thought it might be fun to match up the students for dances or events was also having a go.

The first computerized dating system to enjoy commercial success was founded by Joan Ball in the UK. In the early 1960s Ball got a job in a marriage bureau, but proved so successful at matching couples up that she soon left to start her own. Demand was such that soon she had the idea of using a machine to help. In 1964, she founded the St. James Computer Dating Service, beginning with about 2,500 clients, most of whom were older and either divorced or widowed. She bought time on a mainframe at a computer bureau in order to run the necessary programs, in 1965 changing the company's name to Com-Pat, short for Computerized Compatibility. Ball told the London *Times* that "There is a great need for people to be able to meet others on the same wavelength. Everyone used to mix such a lot more than they do now, in dance halls and social clubs and so on. But now people are more wrapped up in their own worlds: they just go home and watch television. Of course, you can't computerize the chemical thing. The computer isn't clairvoyant and doesn't work miracles." After just three years in business, Com-Pat had matched over 7,000 couples and was later bought out by Dateline, which by the 1980s was the largest computer dating company in the world.

New Scientist, *May 4, 1972*

The contributions of Joan Ball, like those of many pioneering women, have been all but erased from the history of computer dating. Instead, credit is generally given—and stop me if you've heard this one before—to a young, white Harvard dude.

In 1965, a junior math major at Harvard named Jeff Tarr raised $1,250 in a quest, essentially, to meet more girls. Tarr put together one hundred and fifty questions for prospective clients to answer: half about themselves, half about their ideal partner. He called it Operation Match. He paid a friend $100 to write a computer program that matched up couples through the use of an IBM 1401, which they rented from an IBM subsidiary company in nearby Roxbury. All input was on punch cards, all output was printed, and each recipient paid $3 to receive six names.

Operation Match soon attracted the attention of a reporter for the *Boston Globe*. Beneath the headline, "2 Harvard Men Replacing Cupid With Computer," he deemed it "the cleverest business enterprise since J. D. Rockefeller invested in oil." Within six months, Operation Match had received about 90,000 questionnaires and opened offices all over the country to support its Cambridge headquarters. As Jeff Tarr explained, "I wanted people to see Operation Match as a novelty—something neat. I advertised it as a social experiment." Tarr was not the first to have the idea, but his timing and execution improved on earlier attempts. Computer dating seemed largely to avoid any social stigma—perhaps because it was new technology and hence, to college students at least, cool and exciting.

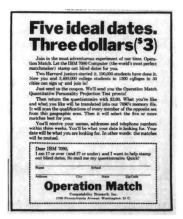

A 1960s advertisement for Operation Match

The founding myth of Operation Match has echoes of Facebook. Both used new technology as a way of replicating the male gaze, offering men access to women without actually having to—horror of horrors—talk to them first. In other words, more sex for less effort. Tarr dictated the questions he deemed important in determining mate choice, and hence he focused on the desires and priorities of a straight white male like himself. It was yet one more way of increasing the power of the already-powerful.

The same year Operation Match launched, an accountant and an IBM programmer teamed up to launch Project TACT (an acronym for Technical Automated Compatibility Testing), New York City's first computer dating service. Clients of Project TACT paid $5 to answer a long questionnaire about likes and dislikes: for women, whether they were most attracted to a man using a power drill, chopping wood, or painting a picture; for men, whether they preferred a Patty Duke bob or a back-combed updo. Then the IBM 1401 printed out five blue cards or five pink cards with potential mates.

In some respects, the early days of computer dating seemed to auger a potentially radical reshaping of the social order. Social conservatives had feared this ever since people of all classes began to advertise for love in the same shared spaces. What actually happened, however, was the opposite.

Historian of technology Mar Hicks has brilliantly demonstrated the way early computer dating operated on one basic principle: it matched up people who were essentially the same in terms of race, religion, and class. Com-Pat brought together Londoners already on the books of a marriage bureau, Operation Match was for college students, and Project TACT targeted Upper East Siders, specifically by tricking doormen into letting them inside the lobbies of the fancier apartment blocks, then writing down the names on everyone's mailboxes. In this way, early computer dating helped uphold the social divide, enforce social hierarchies, and replicate social patterns in the most efficient, data-driven way possible. Not only did early computer dating companies actively seek out white, middle-class users in the hope they would bring with them an air of respectability, but they also focused entirely on the heterosexual community. Structurally incapable of coping with difference, they propagated a fundamentally conservative approach to matchmaking, transferring long-existing social norms onto new technologies in terms of both aims and execution. In other words, they were not nearly as revolutionary as they appeared.

New York's Upper East Side was the testing ground for Project TACT because a large number of single, educated, solvent young women had recently come to reside there; one insurance company estimated (surely generously) that there were 780,000 of them in the neighborhood. "No other parcel of Manhattan real estate is so well geared to the frantic pace of the single girl than" the Upper East Side, according to one fashion magazine. In an article for *Mademoiselle* in 1961, a young Joan Didion commented that those who moved to New York "seem to be girls who want to prolong the period when they can experiment, mess around, make mistakes. In New York, there is no genteel pressure for them to marry, to go two-by-two . . . New York is full of people on this kind of leave of absence."

The same year Project TACT launched, the city's first official singles bar opened. Alan Stillman, a twenty-eight-year-old perfume salesman, was sick of drinking in bars surrounded entirely by men. He decided to buy up his local haunt, a saloon on the corner of East 63rd Street and First Avenue known as the Good Tavern, and make it more female-friendly. He renamed it T.G.I. Friday's, painted the building an enticing bright blue adorned with red-and-white striped awnings, and served up a menu of burgers, beer, and Long Island iced teas in a bright, clean atmosphere. This radical approach proved an instant hit with both the ladies and gents of the neighborhood and beyond (there are now over 1,500 T.G.I. Friday's worldwide).

The United States census of 1960 revealed that eighteen out of every hundred households were headed by women, many of whom enjoyed complete financial independence. Between 1960 and 1970, the female labor force increased by 3.1 percent a year, over three times faster than the male labor force. Job opportunities expanded, although only up to a point. There was a popular board game at the time called What Shall I Be?: The Exciting Game of Career Girls that gave players the option of landing on secretary, teacher, stewardess, model, or nurse; the aim of the game was to avoid becoming an old maid, known as a Dud. The most common profession for women was still a secretary, many of whom lived far from family and friends, were new in town and worked long hours, and perhaps needed a little help in the dating department.

In 1994, thirty-year-old Grateful Dead fan Gary Kremen had an idea that would usher in the most dramatic shift in advertising for love in its history. Kremen was a native of Illinois who then went to Stanford Business School; he won a place on a summer internship at Goldman Sachs, but was so annoying to work with that, after three weeks, one of the partners tried to buy out the rest of his internship if Kremen would agree to resign on the spot. He refused.

Kremen's genius was to put $2,500 on a credit card to register the domain name Match.com (as well as Jobs.com, Housing.com, Autos.com, and Sex.com). Match went live a year later and, in Kremen's first television interview, he boldly declared that it "will bring more love to the planet than anything since Jesus Christ." It was the equivalent of personals in newspapers, but with the added benefit of being searchable. According to the site's first marketing manager, Trish McDermott, "Some argued that we'd never make money, since everyone thought everything on the Internet was supposed to be free. But coming from my old job [running a traditional matchmaking agency in San Francisco], where I saw people pay fifty thousand dollars to find someone, I knew that dating was a unique service."

The problem was that, in 1995, only 5 percent of Americans had access to the Internet. The most popular websites were viewed by 20,000 people a week, the first cyber cafés were just emerging, and an article in Newsweek scoffed at the prospect of online shopping: "Even if there were a trustworthy way to send money over the Internet—which there isn't—the network is missing a most essential ingredient of capitalism: salespeople." Furthermore, the huge majority of those who were online were men; Kremen became so desperate to get more women to sign up to Match.com that he asked his own girlfriend to do so. She did, then promptly left him for someone she met on the website. (The limited reach of this new medium both in terms of numbers and gender recalls the *New England Courant* two hundred years prior, which faced similar challenges.)

Online dating remained a niche enterprise for some years. It proved difficult to obtain venture capital due to the stigma attached; Lois Smith Brady, who oversaw the Vows section of the *New York Times* for many years, recalls that "when I [first] heard about a couple who met online, I wasn't sure I should cover their wedding. It seemed so risky and dangerous. What if other people followed?" It wasn't until Match.com was bought by Barry Diller of conglomerate IAC in 1999 for $50 million that the website really took off, but even Diller truly had no idea of its potential. As Greg Blatt, one of Match's first CEOs, commented, "Back in those days the company was simply buying up a bunch of Internet businesses. Dating just happened to be something that worked out, so we stuck with it."

Today, Match is the largest online dating company in the world. Among its users, 32 percent are Millennials (aged 18–36), 39 percent are Generation X (aged 37–52), and 27 percent are Baby Boomers (aged 53–72), the latter the fastest-growing demographic by far. The site boasts the advantage of being able to track in detail all sorts of user behavior: for example, the search criteria that members say are important to them but most frequently end up ignoring are a) income and b) wanting children. In other words, often we do not know what we want until we see it. The site sees a 60 percent leap in new members signing up between December 25 and February 14, and its web traffic peaks at around 9:00 P.M. on the first Sunday after New Year's Day. These are simply not the kind of statistics that the *New York Herald* in the 1860s was able to track; for the first time, we are faced with a data-driven courtship landscape.

While Match functioned on the principle that users search using minimal filters, later sites did things a little differently. In 2000, clinical psychologist Dr. Neil Clark Warren launched eHarmony, which was the first algorithm-based dating site. Users complete a questionnaire—initially 450 questions, recently reduced to 150—focusing on personality traits, values, beliefs, and so on and are then paired up with other users deemed compatible. In this way, Warren sought to use science to increase the chances of a happy, long-lasting relationship. Within three years, eHarmony boasted over two million registered users.

Focused on marriage specifically, rather than more casual relationships, eHarmony recalled the very earliest personal ads. It functioned like an old-fashioned matchmaker in the way it actively intervened in the courtship process, making judgments on whether two people were suited to each other or not. It also firmly rejected the idea that opposites attract, instead operating under the dubious assumption that couples were happiest when they were as similar to each other as possible.

Other online dating companies quickly emerged to compete with Match and eHarmony. One of the most successful was OkCupid, essentially a cross between the two. Established in 2004 by a math student from Maine named Chris Coyne and two other friends from Harvard, OkCupid allows users to design their own filters to reflect what is and is not important to them, then uses this information to assess potential partners' suitability. "Under 40, not deformed?" Sure. One advantage of this approach is that it minimizes the influence of the straight white patriarchy, aka, the founders of the other sites who designed the algorithms, thereby effectively making space for alternative priorities.

The period between 2005 and 2010 saw the development of the first free dating sites. These relied solely on advertising to make money. By 2011, Plenty of Fish had the most traffic of any dating site in the world and was attracting over six million unique visitors a month. Entirely unregulated or moderated, it was also the spawning ground of more criminal cases than the other dating websites combined.

But advertising for love, sex, or something in between was about to experience a revolution: the smartphone. The earliest smartphone is generally considered to be the Simon Personal Communicator, which IBM put on the market in 1992. Others followed, mostly aimed at business users, and with them the first mobile versions of online dating. In 2003, ProxiDating became one of the earliest adopters of Bluetooth technology to let customers know when a matching profile was physically within fifty feet. Match launched its own mobile version a year later, while other early industry leaders included the likes of WebDate and Lavalife. By the end of 2006, around three million users a month were logging into mobile dating sites, the huge majority of whom were aged under thirty-five.

The launch of the Apple iPhone in 2007 saw these numbers increase exponentially. Today, 77 percent of adults in the United States have a smartphone and there is no need to sneak down to the docks at Peck Slip anymore, like those in the summer of 1788 excited by the prospect of "a young gentleman of fame and fortune . . . not above two and twenty, tall, stout, and esteemed agreeable in his person." A whole world of single men and women is now easily accessible from the dinky device in your back pocket, ever since the 2012 release of location-based dating app Tinder.

Tinder founders Justin Mateen and Sean Rad met in math class during freshman year at the University of Southern California. They have joked that they needed help meeting women, but it is not really a joke. Sex has always been an important driver of technological innovation, it seems (in fact, an important driver of so much).

The genius of Tinder is the swipe, credit for which is generally given to the third person to join the company, Jonathan Badeen, whom Rad met at a tech incubator. According to Badeen, "I was getting out of the shower one morning, wiping the mirror because the room was steamy, and I saw myself staring back at myself. Then I wiped the other direction. All of a sudden it clicked." More cynical onlookers point to his previous work with an app that used flash cards for children to help with their homework, but regardless of origin, the swipe is like turning the page in a newspaper but without the risk of spilling your coffee. It makes the entire experience immeasurably more pleasurable—instinctive, even.

Tinder was an immediate success, producing over 12 million matches a day by the end of 2014. In the beginning, the average user was generally aged between about eighteen and twenty-four (although this demographic quickly expanded) and spent on average an astonishing ninety minutes a day on the app. By the summer of 2018, Tinder had over 3.7 million paid subscribers.

Tinder has since been joined by a number of dating apps that are variations on the same theme. With Bumble, only women can make the first move, while Hinge matches you up with friends of friends or friends of friends of friends and

Happn introduces you to those with whom you have physically crossed paths, for example you have both visited the same coffee shop four times. When analyzed together, they reveal all sorts of fascinating new information about human mate choice: a man who poses for his profile picture with a dog will receive far more matches than anyone else, as will a woman in a yoga pose on a beach.

Dating apps helpfully give you some information about a prospective date in advance, which gives you something to talk about: "Tell me about your dog" or "Do you genuinely like yoga or just think you look good in the outfits?" This form of matchmaking also provides both parties with a sense of what is and is not important to one another, thereby giving the relationship a greater chance of success from the outset: Is it all about money? Is she specifically looking for a brunette? Does he care that she's no good at milking cows? For those with truly niche needs—like the man with a glass eye seeking "a young girl who also has a glass eye or some other deformity not more severe" in the *New York Times* in 1903, for example—it really has proved a godsend.

The Internet is now the number one place where men and women meet. One in three relationships begin online and one in five marriages are a result of a dating website or app. Meanwhile, crimes related to online dating—fraud, theft, even murder, just like during the Gilded Age—leapt by almost 400 percent between 2011 and 2016, and these are the tiny proportion that were reported. Many websites and apps have since improved their safeguarding policies, but the risks remain.

How much, then, has changed in the way we advertise for love?

An ad in an 18th-century newspaper is obviously a very different entity to a profile on a 2020 dating app. Two hundred years ago, those who advertised for love were generally well-off, middle class, white, and (more often than not) male. In contrast, today the process is generally free, available to anyone who is online, and accessible regardless of gender, race, sexuality, religion, or class. It is easier, more convenient, and more inclusive. There is an app for everyone, whatever your predilection. Niche is the new mainstream.

And yet, even more has stayed the same, as is commonplace when human nature is involved.

People still lie, claiming they earn more than they do, weigh less than they do, or are younger than they are.

People still seek access to the lonely and the vulnerable in order to commit crimes.

And, most crucially, people still fall back on many of the same broad criteria when picking a long-term heterosexual partner. We remain depressingly in thrall to the evolutionary demands of human mate choice in the most fundamental way. While of course there are many variations and exceptions, the data shows that most men want women who are fertile, the primary indicator of which is youth; most women want men with resources, enabling them to support any offspring that result from the relationship. Precise definitions of what is meant by this have changed significantly over the years now that women choose to have children later or differently or not at all, as well as to sustain their own financial independence, while men can define resources more broadly than just cash or property by instead including social skills or Instagram followers or the ability to build a campfire when Armageddon comes. The basic principles, however, have stayed intact.

Conclusion

As I write this, my husband is sitting at the desk next to me. Not once today has he mentioned India or suggested a trip to the pub, although he did tell me at breakfast about a new 800-page book about the history of Constantinople that he'd enjoyed. Regardless, he is the one for me.

Why? Why does anyone hitch their lot to anyone? I look around at the couples I know—the happy, the unhappy, the indifferent—and I wonder: Why did she choose him? What does he see in her? Why do we want the one we want? Are they truly the most likely to make us happy?

Whom you choose to marry is arguably the most important decision you will ever make in your entire life—studies show that a happy marriage is by far the strongest predictor of overall happiness—and yet it is so often left to chance. Why not try a more systematic approach? There is no doubt that, in some circumstances, the sorting process is best outsourced.

As the matchmaking process began to flounder as a result of some of the unique challenges faced by 18th- and 19th-century Americans—challenges mostly caused by the presence of either too many people (in the cities) or too few (on the plains and the prairies)—it became clear that many needed or wanted to advertise for love to help them along the road to marriage. Personal ads became a form of public service offered by newspapers, little different to printing the minutes of the town council or letting readers know the deadline for school applications.

Every form of advertising for love has been uniquely shaped by its time and place. The earliest, newspapers, was initially highly class-based, but slowly evolved to meet the demands of a changing America. Come the 20th century, developments like the Pill, the widespread deferment of marriage, the increased number of women in the workforce and the expansion of gay rights all contributed to the merry collapse of many of the conventions of matchmaking. This has led us to the likes of Tinder and beyond, which encourage the user to make rapid responses based predominantly on appearances. These dating apps also have a socially competitive edge to them, thrive on status anxiety, and meet the demand for instant gratification. In other words, they offer up everything deemed important in contemporary culture.

What will be the next iteration of advertising for love? Beaming desires onto the Moon? Neural pathway to neural pathway? In all seriousness, it will be AI. Tinder is already looking into how to use AI to enhance its users' experience. One idea is to introduce computerized personal assistants that have specific responsibility for our dating life: they will match us up, use our online calendars to organize a date, automatically book concert tickets to a band both users like, and probably one day have sex on our behalf, too, so that we humans don't have to bother with that, either. Perhaps the logical conclusion of this sort of dalliance with AI is that eventually we all end up just having a relationship with the computer itself.

The above paragraph will almost certainly have become dated by the time you have finished reading it.

Throughout human history, whenever a new technology has emerged— whether it is the printing press, the silicon chip, or AI—one of the first ways it has been put to use has always been in the forming and facilitation of human relationships, perhaps because this is humans' primary goal. To love and be loved. Isn't that why we are all here? Or, as E. M. Forster (the last person on the planet who would ever have willingly placed a personal ad or used a dating app) put it, "Only connect!"

NOTES ON SOURCES

The vast majority of the material contained in this book is based on primary research conducted at the UCLA Library in Los Angeles, at the British Library in London, and, most of all, using a wide range of online newspaper archives, which are increasing in size and scope with each year that passes and are now almost all searchable. The most useful online newspaper archives included Chronicling America, Newspapers.com, Accessible Archives, and America's Historical Newspapers. These were a crucial source not only of personal ads, but also news stories about personal ads (particularly court cases). I also relied on Ancestry.com to trace some of the people mentioned in the ads.

There are very few secondary sources about the history of personal ads specifically, but Pamela Epstein, "Selling Love: The Commercialization of Intimacy in America, 1860s–1900s" (PhD diss., Rutgers University, 2010) and Marcia A. Zug, *Buying a Bride: An Engaging History of Mail-Order Matches* (New York: New York University Press, 2016) both provided some guidance. See also an earlier book of mine, *Shapely Ankle Preferr'd: A History of the Lonely Hearts Ad* (New York: Vintage Books, 2011), which is about the history of personal ads in Britain.

The material about Johann Hoch in chapter 9 and Belle Gunness in chapter 11 is based on Richard C. Lindberg, *Heartland Serial Killers: Belle Gunness, Johann Hoch, and Murder for Profit in Gaslight Era Chicago* (DeKalb: Northern Illinois University Press, 2011), Sylvia Shepherd, *The Mistress of Murder Hill:*

The Serial Killings of Belle Gunness (Bloomington, Ind.: 1st Book Library, 2001), Janet L. Langlois, *Belle Gunness: The Lady Bluebeard* (Bloomington: Indiana University Press, 1985), and Lillian de la Torre, *The Truth About Belle Gunness* (New York: Fawcett, 1955).

One of the most challenging aspects of researching this book was tracking down real-life couples from the past who met through a personal ad. Edwin L. Lybarger appears in Nancy L. Rhoades and Lucy E. Bailey, eds., *Wanted—Correspondence: Women's Letters to a Union Soldier* (Athens: Ohio University Press, 2009). Sara and Jay Hemsley and Annie and Horace Knapp feature in Chris Enss, *Object Matrimony: The Risky Business of Mail-Order Matchmaking on the Western Frontier* (Guilford, Conn.: TwoDot, 2012), and I found the story about Ole Ruud and Augusta Larson in Esther Ruud Stradling, *American Fever: A Biography of Ole Ruud, Pioneer of the Washington Territory* (Bloomington, Ind.: AuthorHouse, 2004). I am enormously grateful to George Mouchet for his email about his great-grandfather Byron Shaffer, as well as to Linda Vixie for hers about her great-grandfather William Wepsala; thank you both for sharing your family histories so generously with me.

On the subject of advertising for love in the 20th and 21st centuries, I highly recommend Mar Hicks's excellent article "Computer Love: Replicating Social Order through Early Computer Dating Systems" in *Ada: A Journal of Gender, New Media & Technology* (Fall 2016, issue 10); she writes fascinatingly about the sexism inherent in computer dating technology. The quote from Joan Ball is from an interview she gave to the *Times* on March 25, 1972. The article "Romance in the Want Ads" by Patricia Morrisroe in *New York* magazine (March 19, 1984) provided plenty of material, too. Other sources that were especially useful included Dan Slater, *A Million First Dates: Solving the Puzzle of Online Dating* (Carmel, Ind.: Current, 2014), the article "Looking For Someone: Sex, Love, and Loneliness on the Internet" by Nick Paumgarten in the *New Yorker* (July 4, 2011), the article "The Oral History of Tinder's Alluring Swipe Right" by Ben Wiseman in *Wired* (September 28, 2016), and the paper "Disintermediating Your Friends: How Online Dating in the United States Displaces Other Ways of Meeting" by Michael Rosenfeld, Reuben J. Thomas, and Sonia Hausen (*Proceedings of the National Academy of Sciences*, volume 116, issue 36, 2019).

Acknowledgments

Thank you to everyone at Pegasus Books, especially my editor Jessica Case, who has been wonderful in every way.

Thanks, too, to my agent Clare Conville for the happiest of Christmas Eve phone calls.

I am very grateful to Tad Friend, who helped improve this book hugely with his suggestions and input. Elizabeth Day was also an early reader, as well as an ongoing source of strength and encouragement.

I did most of the research for this book while living in Los Angeles. Thank you to my friends there for cheering me along, in particular Jennifer Wilkinson, Sara Lamm, Alexandra Dickson Gray, and Anna Belknap. Meanwhile, I would never have finished writing it without the practical assistance of Mercedes Ancheta, Evie Britton, Tamazin Simmonds, and Susan Bobin, so many thanks to them as well.

My parents Chris and Nicola Beauman have, as always, been enormously helpful and supportive.

And the biggest thanks of all goes to my husband, James Bobin, for—well, for everything.

Finally, I dedicate this book to my children Maddy, Jack, and Wilkie, with much love.